FRANZ SCHUBERT

FRANZ SCHUBERT

From the water-colour by Wilhelm August Rieder (May 1825)

FRANZ SCHUBERT

BY

RALPH BATES

WITH A FRONTISPIECE

PETER DAVIES LIMITED

1934

First published in October 1934

Printed in Great Britain for PETER DAVIES LTD. by T. and A. CONSTABLE LTD.
at the University Press, Edinburgh

To

WINIFRED AND ROSALEEN

FOREWORD

A BRIEF glossary of musical terms will be found at the end of this book. This may be of use to those whose musical knowledge is confined to knowledge of music. If brevity has compelled me to offend by the exclusion of a favourite anecdote, I ask pardon; I also love everything about this man.

R. B.

I

FRANZ SCHUBERT was born in the Lichtenthal suburb of Vienna, in the house of the Red Crayfish, on the 31st of January 1797. It is agreed by shoemakers, barristers' clerks and their historians that their lives are in part shaped by the world into which they are born. In the case of great musicians it is sometimes thought that the rigours of sonata form and the harmonic instability of the minor triad sufficiently account for the vicissitudes they endure. The outline requires filling in, however.

The Vienna of the Schuberts, besides being the city of Mozart and Beethoven, was also of Franz II and Metternich, persons at first haunted by Napoleon, and then by the ideas which had haunted the young Bonaparte.

Joseph II, in the days before the test of the French Revolution, had been a liberal, of the royal sort. He had closed the convents, of which there were 116 in the capital alone and whose total revenue was 680,000 florins annually, given the Prater and the Augarten to the city, and substituted German for Latin as the language of senior education. There is no doubt that some violence accompanied his reforms. Important conventual libraries were burned, so that the world shortly knew less of them than before. Art treasures were damaged by ignorant officials, many of whom resembled later reformers in confusing wrath and love. One of them, indeed, inventoried Titian's Leda as a ' Woman bitten by an angry goose.'

As befitted a liberal the emperor also interfered with the amusements of the people ; he abolished public executions, which were popular, and founded a German opera theatre which was less so. For the former he was lampooned, but no mention was made of the six thousand laws which he signed. His love for music, if limited by his understanding, was genuine, though not so great as that of his successor, Leopold II, who once successfully encored a whole opera.

Leopold, while reactionary, was not sufficiently so to preserve that symmetry observable in the arrangement of the universe. He therefore died within two years, admitting to the throne his son, Franz II. The eternal values now received that fullness of support which it is the heavy responsibility of crowns to provide. The new monarch, as befitted his divine right, did not wholly trust to spies, subsidised sneaks and censorships, nevertheless Beethoven could declare, in 1794, that 'one does not dare to speak too loudly here or the police find one a lodging,' while in 1798 it was reckoned that there were four thousand official spies aiding the ten thousand of the unofficial corporation of the Naderers, informers recruited among servants, waiters, barbers and those of the other occupation thought to provide privileged opportunities for eavesdropping.

Austria was already comparatively inaccessible to revolutionary propaganda. The low standard of intellectual development and a sincere love of pleasure disinclined it for costly and perhaps futile heroisms. Moreover, liberty was chiefly preached in its traditional forms of provincial and district hegemony, and this appealed little to a peasantry who preferred the distant and paternal tyranny of the capital to the more local and less fatherly burden of their own aristocracy. Nor was there any mature sense of nationality to unite the people in a body of common enthusiasm.

But with a wisdom that surpassed liberalism or piety, Franz II desired to make doubly sure. The forces which had secured this immunity were to be reinvigorated. The censorship of the press was reimposed with greater severity and education was once more delivered over to the clergy. The desired result was gained. While German letters at this period could boast of Goethe, Schiller, Fichte and Hegel, the two Schlegels and Humboldt, Austrian fields were almost completely barren of flower. Philosophy, once the pure handmaiden of theology, but now thought to be living in less reputable relationship with revolt, was unrepresented. Science, which is, as has been pointed out by Mr. Chesterton, an affair of mere locomotive speed, vaccination and counterfeit progress, had insecure foothold in Vienna. The pagan century was definitely to be forgotten.

But for this stifling atmosphere there were great compensations. If letters were forbidden as dangerous, music, being innocuous, was encouraged, though had programme music been a flourishing species it is doubtful whether the art would have survived. The innate love of music was fostered by Franz II, himself a passable fiddler, but who saw no conflagration adjacent enough to warrant extending himself. His wife, Maria Theresa, disdaining the milky way to self-expression chosen by another Maria, desired to be an operatic star, and one day created the title rôle in Salieri's *Argina, regina di Granata*.

Music became the very life and atmosphere of the city. Symphonic and chamber music was the delight of an aristocracy distinguished by such unexampled lovers of the art as Lobkowitz, Kinsky and the Archduke Rudolf, who could generously pension the republican Beethoven. The waltz, the ländler and the march were not less popular with other classes. Yet in all this fervour and delight of music-making it is worth while to notice that of all the eminent composers who practised in Vienna only one was native born, Franz Schubert.

One other result of governmental severity must be mentioned because without it the life of Schubert is unintelligible. Besides music, pleasure became the prevailing passion of the Viennese, and Pleasure, as the little confessional books one meets in port missions indicate, is a music which eternally harps back to two themes. Chastity, as every healthy male knows who has lived in a country whose pre-

vailing outlook is not a dreary puritanism, is
a virtue, fact or hindrance easily mislaid. The
gaiety and comfortable humour of the Gasthaus
often encouraged a certain naturalism in behaviour. Vienna, indeed, became a place of
diverting licence in which scandal and intrigue,
natural enough where one-third of the city at
one time lived at the expense of the court or
the imperial kitchen, received fresh motives
for exercise.

Hence, when the sober and pious Franz
Theodor Florian Schubert came to Vienna as
an assistant teacher to his brother Karl, it was
to a city of peril as well as of opportunity that
he came. The fifth son of a righteous Moravian, a former magistrate, he had been
brought up in an atmosphere of comparative
poverty and incomparable moral rigour. It
is easy to imagine that his father's office compelled a circumspection which, if it did not
provoke rebellion, would encourage every
element of sternness and domination which
the boy possessed. And he was stuffed full of
them.

It may have been the hated military service
which impelled Franz Theodor to choose the
teaching profession, the army being then ill-
clothed and paid, starved, perplexed with

disease, fleshliness and the brimstone vice.
The minor importance of the elected profession may have attracted the magistrate's son.
This alone would have prompted him to become a priest, but it is possible that he was
well aware that his sexual appetite was too
vigorous for voluntary emasculation. At any
rate, soon after being appointed to the head-
mastership of the Lichtenthal school upon the
significant recommendation of a bishop, he
married Elizabeth Vitz, a cook, seven years
older than himself. His wife's age and his
own extreme poverty suggest an urgent maturity in the young man of twenty-two. Fourteen
children were born of the marriage, the first,
Ignaz, in 1784, after which the almost yearly
birth was accompanied by yearly death.
Schoolmaster Schubert was a person of extreme
discipline, with that moral knack of fusing
love and hate into one decision which renders
the will inflexible, but this procreativeness,
persisted in despite annual loss, could not have
been only to satisfy the ever-repeated injunc-
tion of a clergy, however venerated. Nor was
there any question of outbreeding heresy in
those days. Everything argues that the father
of the musician was a man of imperative sexual
need, which in conjunction with a piety which

amounted to bigotry, despotic intolerance and a hunger and thirst after success and respectability, made him recoil in distrust from the city that lay across the green Glacis from Lichtenthal. So that, despite a modest love of music, in which, however, his three sons surpassed him, he also hated music. That is to say, he dreaded its influence, the life it encouraged and the moral dubiety of the circles in which its secular practitioners moved. Very little will be understood of the relationship between Schoolmaster Schubert and his son Franz if it is not realised that his objection to the career of music was not entirely economic ; especially as the freedom of enjoyment discoverable in the city was ever a taunt and a jibe to the hungry flesh turned moralist in him. The grimness, not tempered by but admitting love, which he manifested later, resembles protestantism rather than catholicism. He had, indeed, acquired the protestant vision of success as the compensation for morality.

Everything points to the father's homogeneity of character. The very profession of his wife was an asset to one whose school permitted boarders. When she died he promptly remarried, and as was to be expected, chose a woman twenty years younger than himself, the submissive daughter of a comfortable silk-manufacturer.

He was capable of philanthropic action, which he wisely confined to the organising of a benevolent society within his profession and to giving free lessons at his school, which badly needed to live down its former evil reputation. He was capable and indefatigably hard-working, so that from no pupils at all the attendance at Lichtenthal at length reached three hundred. This, however, did not lift him above a poverty which became so oppressive that in 1796 he applied for another post. He was refused, the government officials informing him that great men must be without ambition. They had acquired this knowledge introspectively, but the method has since been discredited.

Two years before this rebuff the Schoolmaster's children had begun to survive, which prompts one biographer to remark that perhaps the recent mortality was providential, for a year later, and in strict defiance of the theory of eugenics, Franz Peter was born and duly baptized. His patron saint was to be Francis the Seraphic, guardian of the interests of schoolmasters.

It was from the Schoolmaster himself that

Franz, a happy, play-loving boy of eight years, received his first instruction in violin playing. Brother Ignaz, the hardened and secret sceptic of the family, later gave him pianoforte lessons, and has recorded his astonishment when, at the end of a few months, the boy announced that henceforth he would not need his instruction. Franz was next placed for musical studies with Michael Holzer, organist of the Lichtenthal church. This implies no weakening of the father's resolve that Franz, like his other sons, should become a teacher. The posts of parish organist and teacher were usually filled by the same person.

Michael Holzer was a sound teacher within his natural limits, a fine drinker and an even more excellent man of the heart, who carried his wine so well that he knew good music from bad even when drunk. This is excellent ; it is even more pleasant to remember that Holzer was then in his seventies. He was, of course, fat, cheerful and sentimental, and recognising the genius of his pupil, often besought the Schoolmaster, doubtless with tears in his eyes and a muttered curse on pickled herrings, to let the boy embark upon a musical career. It is to be feared that the sweet odour of insanctity in his breath sometimes robbed his arguments of their force.

II

WHEN Franz reached the age of eleven years
and eight months a place for one soprano
became vacant in the Chapel Royal. This
post carried with it the obligation of attendance at the Convict, an important Jesuit
college, and accordingly the Schoolmaster
entered his son for the examination. As a
disciplinary preparation for the then joyless profession of teaching the Convict would be ideal.

Dressed in the cheap grey smock of the
working classes, Franz was derisively described
by his fellow competitors at the examination
as the son of a miller, but the boy who was
later to raise millers to a notable place in art
carried all before him with the fine quality of
his voice, already of local fame, and the
thoroughness of his knowledge. At the end
of 1808 he put off the smock for the discreetly
gay uniform of the Convict.

The Convict building in which Schubert
was now to live justified the inescapable sug-
gestiveness of its name, being a repellent and

gloomy place of draughts and discomfort. The
school had been closed by Joseph II in the
course of a dispute with the Jesuit superiors,
in which the emperor was probably blame-
worthy, the Order of Jesus having then, as
now, an uncanny skill in putting its enemies
in the wrong. Franz II, disapproving of pre-
judice, had reopened the school after minor
provision of reform.

Despite the rigorous conditions, not entirely
new to him, there is no doubt that Schubert
was on the whole happy at the Convict. His
character appeared to change, however. Formerly gay and spontaneous, he now became
quiet and reserved, showing for the first time
the inveterate shyness which was to be his
severest handicap and which is so psychologic-
ally revealing. It was not a question of mis-
anthropy or the Beethoven scowl, he was
simply rendered mute by the suddenly released
upsurge of unceasing musical experience
within him, which in Schubert seems to have
taken the place of that reverie in which the
rest of us express our unrecognised Napole-
onic, Messianic or Casanovian qualities.
Friendship, of a discriminated kind, was from
the very first more important to him than
any other thing, save music.

There was almost unlimited opportunity for both vocal and instrumental music at the Convict, which also taught something of the other necessities of life. The most just of judgments upon Dr. Lang, the principal, is that he appears to have been a close relative of the well-known Dr. Fell. He was severe, stiff and contemptuous of children, but not greatly unpopular until later. The chief musical instructor was Salieri, Beethoven's friend and one-time teacher, a brilliant and lazy dictator in decline, not so sinister as he appears in Pushkin's play based on Mozart's assertion that he had been poisoned by him, but not over-scrupulous in the performance of his duties, and embittered against modern music. He disliked Beethoven's work and detected faults in *Figaro*, a sin that inclines one to get up and hoot him down without hearing. As Salieri has been treated with both excessive scorn and leniency, it is as well to close with him at once.

The greatest harm he did to Schubert was to fire his imagination with thoughts of writing opera. Himself a moderately competent opera writer and fellow-countryman of the prodigiously successful Rossini, his promptings of the penniless and hungry boy need not have

been very insistent, for a series of successful
opera was about the only way to prosperity at
the time. He approved Schubert's first operatic work, which bore the lusty title of *The
Devil's Castle of Pleasure*, and may thus have
confirmed him in an affair of tragic waste,
nor did he give his pupil any serious instruction in dramatic writing. The truth is that
Salieri had nothing much to teach, even in
opera. One of the most venerable of author-
ities on Schubert's music has argued otherwise,
chiefly upon the strength of Beethoven's
Variations on an air of Salieri's, *La Stessa,
la stessima*, all the dramatic fitness of which
air turns out to be merely a matter of panto-
mimic possibility. To read through his Cesares
and Palmiras is to discover plenty of music which
Sir Thomas Beecham could make sound like a
lesser man's performance of Rossini, but little
of characterisation, certainly nothing remotely
approaching the amazing subtlety of *Figaro*.
And it was *Fidelio* which should have been the
model for the romantically inclined Schubert.

Salieri also tried to dissuade Schubert from
the writing of songs, but without effect. It
is just possible that this might have been bene-
ficial to the Schubert of the larger forms, but
it would have been an incomparable loss to

music. Salieri, moreover, advised his pupil
against setting Goethe's verse. He placed
before the boy the scores of Gluck and balanced
this good by insisting that he should study the
scores of Corelli and the mosaical Italians,
who must have appeared to Franz to have
' worked very well with ideas they had not.'
It must be placed to Salieri's credit that
Schubert obtained leave to take exterior
lessons in thoroughbass, for this was a rarely
granted privilege. The boy's musical education undoubtedly was not of desirable thoroughness, but the fault most likely lay in entrusting
what Salieri probably thought a minor task to
one of the principal musical figures of the day,
engaged in the distracting ceremonial life of
the court. Moreover, it must have been
difficult to direct the studies of a boy who
always appeared to have mastered everything
previously, and Ruziczka and Holzer both
testify to this. The severest judgment on the
Italian is that which has been held to be his
chief extenuation. He did not profoundly
influence his pupil. His best defence is that
he sometimes treated the boys to ice-cream.
There was really only one possible teacher for
the young Schubert, and that one also impossible, the deaf Beethoven.

The Convict's singing master was the yellow-faced, wizened and pig-tailed Korner, a vaguely important musical bully, a kind of beadle to Salieri, the pianoforte teacher being Ruziczka, a genial Moravian of strongly national tastes in music. At this time this must have meant contact with the folk music of rural Austria; the delightful ländler and waltzes of Schubert may owe something to Ruziczka's enlightened enthusiasm.

If Franz's mental life was filled with serenity, his material existence was in sufficient contrast. Food was poor and scanty, and in 1812 he wrote, not to his father, but to Ferdinand, Big Brother Ferdinand : 'You know by experience how sometimes one wants to eat a roll and a few apples and all the more when after a modest dinner one can only look forward to a wretched supper eight and a half hours later.' He asks for a few kreuzers a month, quotes the Bible in support of charity and closes pleadingly.

Besides hunger there was an atmosphere of tyranny to breathe. Franz himself never once earned punishment, and the sweetness of his character was even commented upon by his teachers. But good behaviour was insufficient defence at the Convict. Max Spaun, brother of Franz's lifelong friend Joseph, received such brutal treatment from his theological instructors that he begged Joseph to be present at his examination. The brother consented, but fled from the classroom at the spectacle of the cruelty displayed by the teacher. Max begged in vain to be allowed to leave the school, and was twice brought back after escape. No doubt he was a weakly neurotic boy who had not read the idealistic treatises on school management which the Order of Jesus had to its credit, for long afterwards when, like his brother, he had risen to importance, Max still could not set eyes on the Convict without distress.

Life at the Convict was not without major excitement. During the six-hour siege of Vienna in 1809, the pupils watched the flaming projectiles stream across the reddened sky. One shell fell into the square before the school and exploded in the basin of a fountain, another crashed through the roof and two storeys of the Convict and burst in the prefects' room. Unfortunately, according to next morning's student comments, the prefects were absent. Previously to this Dr. Lang had made himself unpopular by forbidding the pupils to enlist in the Students' Defence Corps. When

25

they defied him and returned beribboned and excited to fill the hollow corridors with their patriotic shouts, he drove them to their rooms and eventually called in one of the Archdukes, a more naturally persuasive antagonist of their exaggerated patriotism. There were plenty of defenders outside without the intervention of little trebles, for the population had half-heartedly rallied. No doubt the emperor first promised them an end to all previous hardships and then, after the Peace, a return to pre-war prosperity.

After brief occupation of Vienna Napoleon departed, and music seemed even sweeter consolation for a life of hunger in a bankrupt, terrorised and counterfeit city.

III

Besides singing in the choir Schubert performed in the school orchestra, in part formed of those whose voices had broken. Holzapfel, his earliest friend, gives a pleasant picture of Schubert fagging as orchestra librarian, dodging among the music desks distributing score, sticking candle-stumps in the greasy sconces, and then hurrying back to his place behind Spaun, the first violin. Such was the excellence of his playing that in the absence of Ruziczka he was entrusted with the baton.

The music played included symphonies of Haydn and Mozart, the overture to *Figaro* which, excepting that to the *Magic Flute*, Schubert thought the loveliest in the world, overtures by Mehul and Boieldieu and works by Krommer and Kozeluch, which latter he preferred to Krommer's cheerful material. This preference is suggestive; Krommer was the more vigorous of the two, Kozeluch being an adherent of the older style. Examining the scores of Kozeluch it is difficult to see any-

27

thing warranting enthusiasm nowadays. Of
three pianoforte sonatas I like best the first,
the opening movement of which would be
well worth playing. It should be added that
the symphonies of Beethoven very soon awakened enthusiasm in Schubert. The enormous
musical significance of this will be developed
later.

In vocal music the popular Zumsteeg became his model, not altogether unfortunately.
Far too much attention has been paid to the
externalities of such productions as the *Ritter
Toggenburg Ballad* which Zumsteeg began in
G Major and at great length brought to a
close in A♭ Major, and the thirty pages of
Die Entführung, like nothing so much as one
of Mr. Ramsay MacDonald's more serious
periods. Zumsteeg's modulations may have
influenced Schubert, but more important is
the fact that his music is definitely German in
feeling and style, continuing in this respect
the campaign against the Italian domination.
A *Nachtgesang*, though exceedingly clumsy,
is melodic in his disciple's manner. The
initial phrase of the *Via Crucis* is strong,
though obvious, and *The Parson's Daughter
of Taubenhagn*, though it lacks the cheerful
entertainment of a version I know in English,

begins with a phrase in F Minor which certainly shows the new influence.

Music was the all-important matter for
Franz now. Soon after entering the Convict
he had begun to compose, upon paper which
Spaun supplied to the penniless lad, appre-
hensively imposing secrecy upon those friends
in whom he confided. The Schoolmaster must
not be allowed to hear of it.

But the Schoolmaster did find out, presumably because Franz was neglecting his
other studies. The father's behaviour on
discovering this iniquitous neglect was true
to type and the Theory of the Family. In
order to prove that, if paternity is a less
material fact than maternity, it is nevertheless a morally superior one, he banished
Franz from the house, without permitting
him to take leave of his mother. After which
one would not be surprised to discover that
Schubert Vater practised the *couvade*.

There can be no doubt that this was grievous
to Franz ; every picture of him given by his
friends at the Convict shows him to have been
a quiet, sensitive, deeply affectionate and
pure-hearted boy of exactly that introspective
kind that would feel the hurt most deeply and
brood over it to his harm. Indeed, early in

1811, among his first compositions we find a setting of a long morbidly worded composition called *The Parricide* portraying the remorse and eventual insanity of the criminal, concluding with an address to conscience. Boyish tastes considered (he had already composed a Corpse Fantasia), it may be unwise to see in this any kind of reaction to his banishment. There is, however, incontrovertible evidence that at a later date he felt the rupture profoundly. In 1822, upon reconciliation after another quarrel, he wrote the allegorical fragment known as ' My Dream.'

' I was one of many brothers and sisters. We had a good father and mother. I felt a deep love for them all. One day my father took us to a feast. My brothers became very merry there, yet I remained sad. My father therefore came to me and ordered me to taste the delicious foods. But I could not, and so my father in anger banished me from his sight. I turned on my heel and with a heart filled with immense love for those who scorned it, wandered into a far country. For years I was torn between the greatest of loves and the greatest sorrow.'

He speaks of reconciliation under circumstances to be recounted shortly, and describes his return to the home which he calls 'the garden.'

'Then one day my father led me again into his pleasure-garden. He asked me if it pleased me. The garden was hateful to me and I dared not reply. Then he asked me a second time . . . tremblingly I told him No, at which my father struck me and I fled.'

A visionary maiden, out of whose tomb bright sparks unceasingly coruscated in a shower upon several young men, though not upon the old, eventually and in a perplexing manner brought him to his father's arms. His father wept, 'and I still more,' concludes the fragment.

Death is a persuasive teacher, and so in March 1812 the Schoolmaster was moved to forgive his son. They were reconciled, but at the death-bed of the boy's mother, who died on the 12th of that month. Uninvited, Franz had returned to say farewell to the dying woman.

Among the twenty-one compositions of the following year is a cantata for his father's name-day festival, which may have touched his heart. The boy himself seems to have thought there was something remarkable in his com-

posing this cantata, for the manuscript of the
verses bears the inscription ' For my father's
name-day ! ! ! '

In this year, however, the Schoolmaster
guardedly compromised in permitting Franz
to undertake more serious studies with Salieri,
probably at Ruziczka's instance. Schubert
now began to frequent his home, and there is
a delicate account of him playing in the home
quartet and gently correcting his father's not
infrequent mistakes at the 'cello desk. The
first time the error occurred Franz would say
nothing, but at a repetition there would be a
discreet tap and a murmured ' Sir, I believe
something here might be improved upon.'
The Schoolmaster was a well-disciplined man,
and it would have taken considerably more
than mere accuracy to deflect his will from the
path of virtue. He accepted such reproofs
pleasantly enough. From these years date the
first string quartets of Schubert, written for
the family.

During this student period and through the
kindliness of Spaun, Franz became acquainted
with opera. *The Swiss Family* of Weigl he
liked, the *Medée* of Cherubini, *Jean de Paris* of
Boieldieu, the *Magic Flute*, and the *Iphigenia in
Tauris* of Gluck filled him with joy and adora-

tion of the singer Vogl, who was later to return the homage of service to the song-writer.

Schubert's voice had already broken and settled into a weak tenor when at the end of October 1813 he left the Convict. He now entered the St. Anna Training College, and having yielded to his father's reasonable warnings about the destitution of a musician's life, began to train for the seraphic profession, at which he was to earn thirty-two shillings a year in cash.

IV

In his dealings with Franz the Schoolmaster
had now a powerful ally in the State, for in
1814 Schubert was presented with his first
conscriptive call to the Austrian colours.
Beethoven had declared that if only he understood the art of war as he did the science of
music he would soon have put down the
renegade Napoleon ; but Schubert's was not
that kind of music. Having qualified for the
post he entered his father's school, now at
Saülengasse, as assistant teacher upon receiving his third call to the service, thus securing
exemption. He cannot be seriously blamed
for this evasion ; he was not to know that the
Congress of Vienna, with which the campaign
was to terminate, was to do so much for the
cause of dancing, and by implication, music.

The following three years' exercise of his
profession must have been hateful to him
and upon occasion mercilessly crushing. The
work was continuous and difficult and con-
ducted in depressing conditions. The small

house, with its low ceilings and little ventila-
tion, must have been the worst possible place
for a school of more than three hundred pupils.
Ignaz says of Franz that he was delivered over
like a beast of burden to the grossest impertin-
ences of youth, in addition to which he was at
the mercy of an ungrateful public and the
imbecile *bonzes*. The word ' bonzes ' pours a
flood of light upon the atmosphere existing in
the family circle. The adjective makes it
clear that Ignaz is here referring to the education bureaucracy, but normally the word
denoted the clergy, especially the higher ranks.
It was a favourite term with Ignaz, who, being
of the same dour metal as his father, was able
to accept the relentless discipline of Saülengasse without open insurrection, but secretly
satisfied rebellious instincts by rejecting the
Schoolmaster's religion.

A letter of Ignaz, dated 1818, discloses the
state of affairs in the schools consequent upon
the Decree of 1806, which gave the clergy
increased powers of control. The occasion
was the feast day of St. Francis the Seraphic.
In the morning the pupils confessed, after
which they were assembled before the altar
of the saint, at the sides of which students'
banners were draped. ' Then followed a little

sermon in which we were told that we must
learn to distinguish evil from good and to
honour the painstaking Schoolmaster. After
which we recited a new-fangled litany to the
saint.' A relic of this same saint was then
presented to the assembly to be kissed. Here
Ignaz makes the acute observation that at
this point many adults sidled towards the
door, adding ' perhaps they had small desire
to participate in that grace.'

The letter concludes with a strophe of the
poet Bürger (whose *Little Village* Schubert
set to music), a free translation of which would
be, ' Don't envy the cohort of bonzes their
venerable heads, the greater part of which are
as empty as the clappers of their belfries.' A
postscript warns Franz against an earlier indiscretion. ' If you write to father and to me
in the same letter do not mention religious
matters.'

Franz replied : ' Ignaz, you are still the
same old man of iron. Your implacable hatred
of all the swarm of bonzes is a credit to you.
You haven't an idea, though, of what the
priests are like here.' (He was then in Hungary.) ' Bigoted as cattle, stupid as jackasses
and graceless as oxen . . . they hurl from
the pulpit such expressions as " worthless

wretches " and " rabble " until it is a pleasure
to listen to them. Or they hold up a skull and
say, " Look at this, freckled mugs, you'll be
like this some day," or again, " Look at that
lad going into the pub with his wench. They'll
dance all night and then fall into bed together,
quite tight. Soon there'll be three of them." '

This letter, the first half of which is also
addressed to Ferdinand and his wife but
which could not be shown to the father, makes
it easy to imagine the family sitting round the
table after school, the Schoolmaster comment-
ing upon the day's work, Franz barely pre-
tending to listen, aching with the throb of
frustrated music in his brain, Ferdinand, large
of spirit, easily concurring or faintly smiling
when, irritated by a pious phrase from his
father, Ignaz indulged in some veiled sarcasm.
Ferdinand was not to rebel ; he was also a
composer and wrote masses, sensibly and com-
fortably, not with the distress of genius but
with enough of mental sweat to deepen his
love for Franz and to earn its lifelong return.

It cannot be doubted that Schubert adopted
the iron brother's anti-clericalism, for such it
was rather than irreligion, and that this was
not entirely the result of personal disposition
but of reaction to the Schoolmaster. That

Franz received a 'moderate' in divinity (which was classed as theoretical religion) and a 'bad' in practical religion upon leaving the St. Anna Training College is indication of distaste for such exercises, although all his life he retained a deep nature-mysticism which might well have been exercised within the Church.

This indistinction was certainly not the result of inability or general indifference, for he secured 'good' and 'fair' in all other subjects, while formerly the emperor himself had remarked upon his deficiencies outside of music.

The music of this period is an aid to understanding. In 1814 Schubert composed his Mass in F, the first of six and the one in which he most nearly achieves the profoundest essence of catholic worship. That essence is, of course, not really expressible in accented and non-contrapuntal music, as doctors teach, though the Holy Ghost, presumably the inspirer of music, has not always been aware of the fact, to judge by the beauty of many of these non-polyphonic masses.

The Mass in F is reverent and mystical in a reasonable fashion, and it happens to be the only one in which the text of the Office is employed with any precision.

Now this mass was composed for Holzer's

choir at the parish church of Lichtenthal, and its composition had the approval and encouragement of the Schoolmaster, who presented Franz with a five-octave piano after its performance. The work was thus written in part for a friend and without the usual embitterment. For a while the warmth of filial love glowed freely within Franz's heart and the mass was a success. The great Salieri, who was present, went round boasting that Schubert was his pupil.

The point can be pursued in detail without any forcing of the facts. The Mass in F is a distinctly individual work, while the next two are not. There is comparatively little trace of Mozart and Haydn in it, whereas the B♭ and G Major masses are saturated with older influences. The *Credo* is especially noteworthy. Schering makes the observation in his *Messe und Requiem seit Haydn und Mozart* that Schubert was the first to achieve the form which is now considered most proper. The principal subject of the *Credo* does not return until the *Et in Spiritum*, this being the procedure which Beethoven adopted for the Missa Solemnis, while in his C Major Mass he followed the old models.

The *Credo*, then, was a part of the canon

to which Schubert paid special attention in 1814. All the later masses, written in 1815, 1819-1822 and 1828, make such astonishing omissions in the text of the *Credo* as to reduce the meaning of several important clauses to complete nonsense. ' Confiteor,' sings the choir,—' confiteor unum baptisma in remissionem peccatorum mortuorum.' ' I confess one baptism for the remission of dead sins.' The omission of the resurrection clause occurs in all the remaining masses, with other errors of the kind. There is no need to make more of this than a failure to keep liturgical contact with the Church, though, if it were desired, one has to hand the fantastic chance that in the A♭ Mass of 1819-1822, which despite its transitional nature is perhaps the most mystical of them all, the words ' Patrem omnipotentem ' are also omitted. Had Schubert been composing in the Seville of this period he might have been saved from the Inquisition only by the fact that the ' atheistic and masonic ' Constitution of Cadiz was just then demanding the suppression of the Holy Office. The grandeur of the E♭ Mass, written in the summer of 1828, a few months before his death, has been taken to prove that Schubert was still a devout Catholic. In that summer he composed a psalm, in Hebrew, for the synagogue in Vienna, and though the Jews, wretched and mercenary race, even paid for the music as was their custom, this was a thing that no sound churchman would do, even in a forgetful moment.

The mass to Schubert was a great musical form of a kind that might secure performance. If his work in that form is often filled with deep feeling, it is for the reason that its imagery, its solemnity and drama awakened the profound mysticism in him, as it does in most of us, a mysticism which probably he mistakenly thought the better part of religion. From the Church and the rigours of a family which reproduced in miniature the State, he reacted, not to a defiant or easy unbelief, nor like a modern poetaster to a Waste Land of Straw Men (the musician was of a stuff less subject to windy variability), but creatively, with a greater love for music. In that music he made his spiritual revaluation, not of the heroic passions, but of the normal qualities, of love, friendship, ease, *gemütlichkeit*, sorrow and joy, which is what makes him the musician beloved of the unheroic, unlearned man in the street ; for he, poor devil, rebels in his own way against living in a street.

41

V

THE external facts of Schubert's life during these three years are simple enough. Gradually he was drawing round him that remarkable circle of friends from which his later life is inseparable. His Convict acquaintances sometimes visited the Saülengasse school, to the severe displeasure of the father, while Franz, defying the prohibition of Dr. Lang, returned their calls at the Convict. Upon Sunday afternoons, when the students were compelled to attend a service, they were accustomed to lock the musician in one of the common rooms, with sufficient music paper to occupy his time. Compositions invariably resulted. Spaun still purchased the paper which Schubert was unable to afford.

In 1814 Schubert also made the acquaintance of the widow Grob and her daughter Theresa, at whose musical parties Salieri and Holzer both attended. Had there been no other interest, the spectacle of these two disputing over music in itself must have dispersed the tedium of ceremony. Theresa Grob, plain-faced and pock-marked, but a singer of rare quality, who had performed the soli of the Mass in F at Lichtenthal church, at once began to attract Franz.

That the two fell sincerely in love is certain from the declaration which Schubert made several years later, though it was spoken to a bosom friend at evening time, while walking in a forest, circumstances helpful to the discovery of blighted passions. They might have married had Schubert possessed an income, but the prospects of an assistant teacher who took no great pains to hide his determination to become a musician would never have satisfied the widow, a merchant with small properties. More exemplary in obedience than Franz, Theresa eventually married a master baker at the request of her mother.

Hope of marriage to Theresa may have prompted the unsuccessful application for a post at the Laubach School of Music which Schubert made in April 1816, though this fusion of music and the profession of his father's unrelenting will would have been comforting to him, as the Mass in F reveals. Schubert was continually dreaming of escape from Saülengasse ; that he contemplated effecting

43

it by means of another academic appointment argues the intensity of the desire.

Only one significant reference to marriage occurs in Schubert's scanty writings. His diary unfortunately fell into the hands of an autograph dealer who sold leaf by leaf what must have been of immense importance not only to biographers, but to all who would understand the fascinating problem of musical creation. The few sheets that remain are of surprising interest.

His diary for the 8th of September 1816 contains a few not very remarkable reflections on the theme of ' all the world's a stage,' in which the most suggestive lines are ' Surely a player has never been dismissed . . . because he spoke his lines badly ? As soon as he gets a suitable rôle he will play it well.' Some stinging taunt from the Schoolmaster may have met its answer here, undelivered elsewhere because throughout his life Schubert was diffident of speech. Then follows this passage :

' Happy moments lighten the sadness of life. Up in heaven these radiant moments will turn into joy perpetual and even more blessed will be the vision of worlds more blest,' etc. The compression of all that glory

of the Mystic Rose and the cloud upon cloud
of incandent seraphs crying eternally, etc.,
into that prosaic summary, probably indicates
that Schubert was recalling some homily, as
the somewhat meaningless formula also suggests. But the thought beneath was sincere
and provoked the haste which resorted to the
recollection. The next passage then is also to
be taken seriously.

' Happy is he who finds a trusty friend.
Happier still is he who finds a true friend in
his wife. Nowadays the thought of marriage
is full of terrors for a single man. He sees it
only as dreariness or wanton sensuality.
Monarchs of to-day, you see this and are
silent ! or do you fail to see it ? ' The defini-
tion of a friend was one who understood music,
and Theresa was one such, but it is surely
unusual in a lad of nineteen to see such an
apposition in marriage, certainly when he is
pining for union with a beloved. The dreariness would, I take it, result from the diminished sexual excitement which marriage is
supposed to involve, as seems clear from his
apposition. A normal youth rejects all asser-
tions that sexual appetite can diminish while
yet manhood lasts as cynicisms, ignoble ones,
if with reference to a lover. Such dread of

marital boredom is rather a sign of maturity, or at least of the experiences which accompany it. If not this, it indicates a strongly nomadic sexual temperament. As it seems unlikely that Franz had already experienced the sweetest delight of the flesh, the dismay, almost disillusion, of his thought must therefore have root in some other maturity, brought about by the sublimation or catharsis of desire, such as the creative activity of blazing genius.

When one regards the astonishing pouring out of music throughout this period it is almost impossible to believe he could have the time at his disposal. The year of his study at the St. Anna College produced a full-length mass, two string quartets in D and B♭ (numbers 7 and 8), a three-act opera of 341 pages of full score, a quantity of songs and other vocal music, including the perfect *Gretchen am Spinnrade*. 1815 brought slavery, and by March the Second Symphony in B♭, a Mass in G, and the Ninth String Quartet in G Minor. The Third Symphony in D also dates from this summer. In the autumn another mass was created : minor Church compositions and other choral works, three one-act operas and one of two acts, an unfinished sonata, and other pianoforte works still left time for 144 songs, one of which was the *Erlking*. Next year saw two more symphonies, one being the delightful Fifth in B♭ Major ; another Mass in C ; the three exquisite violin and pianoforte sonatas ; and an unfinished opera in three acts, besides more than a hundred songs, including the massive *An Schwager Kronos*.

The manner of composition is even more interesting than the quantity. The manuscript allegro of the B♭ Quartet, Opus 168, bears the limiting times of its composition. It was written in four and a half hours, hardly time to copy it. The manner in which the *Erlking* was *whelmed* down on paper is everyone's knowledge. It lends plausibility to Vogl's fanciful claim that Schubert's music was a product of clairvoyance. Many works literally burst from the man without premeditation and with rarely a moment's thought for them once they were finished. The output of July 1815, twenty songs, is nothing beside that of one day, 19th October, eight songs ; and this is not his record.

All this is compulsive to belief ; common terms and estimates do not apply to such phenomena. The man's whole life had become music. Turned back from the visible world, he did not laboriously construct a world of thought, or thought-music, but serenely stepped over into a shining world of loveliness and liberty with an athleticism of spirit the like of which had been witnessed only once before, in the person of Mozart.

Or rather, this was not witnessed. Apart from the songs, it is true to say that Schubert never heard his greatest works with the fleshly ear. At this period only a few friends even so much as saw the scores, other than the quartets composed for the family quartet and the orchestra which grew out of it. Until the end of the Saülengasse years Schubert had never received a penny for his music, and it was long after that his so-called Opus 1, the *Erlking*, was published. He never boasted of his creativeness ; his friends called upon him at his room, and there were the manuscripts, lying around in confusion, or thrust into drawers, forgotten, their purpose fulfilled. So careless was he that his manuscripts became the prey of connoisseurs ; at one time a certain Pinterics claimed dozens of such ' possessions.' Thus were many works irretrievably lost.

The manuscript of Six Ecossaises bears the

inscription ' Composed while a prisoner in my own room. Thank God.' A practical joke by his friends, symbolic of the shutting out of the world, and he turned to music and was grateful for the imprisonment.

But this period of constraint was rapidly drawing to a close. Schubert's circle of friends was extending. Spaun had introduced him to admirers, a friend had given him Mayrhofer's poem *Am See*, the poet himself he met after setting the words. Schober, his lifelong companion, now came within the net of his personality. The freedom of the music-loving, pleasure-seeking city across the Glacis was irresistibly magnetic to one so confined.

Nor was the quivering impetus of music within any longer to be held in check. The composition of essays in the comedy of manners, such as with important reservations his early instrumental works were, could no longer satisfy his genius, aflame with new romantic impulses. A comparison of the quartets written for home performance and the straining lyricism of the 1817 pianoforte sonatas tells the tale more aptly than biography. Franz's ambitions meant taking music seriously, and in the next room the Schoolmaster was drowning his thoughts with angry prayers to St. Francis the Seraphic.

He abandoned his profession. Some time in 1817 Franz Schubert escaped into the city, shot off like a strange alpha-particle from the inert mass of Saülengasse.

VI

It was to Schober that Franz first went for
asylum, and then to the house of the brilliant
and provocative historian, Professor Watteroth,
a man acclaimed by his pupils and detested
by the Church for his defence of heresy ; in
sum, a minor and very amiable Voltaire.
For this Wattrot, as Schubert spells the name,
he had already composed a name-day cantata,
since lost, upon the appropriate theme of
Prometheus, receiving for it as his first professional payment the sum of £4.

Franz had left the house of one pedagogue to
enter that of another, but one conspicuous for
humane friendship and his flouting of the Schoolmaster's church. It is not the only significance
discoverable in his behaviour of these years.

His remarks upon marriage are followed by
a curious reference to monarchs. In effect,
he expresses a wish that Franz II, of all people,
should put an end to that apposition between
boredom and sensuality. It is similar to the
preceding entry in being clearly a remembered

fragment of some conversation with a group of doctrinaire radicals. Those familiar with the politics of a Catholic country will hear in the passage an echo of the endless tirades of club, tavern and Athenaeum against the excessively biological and material conception of marriage and the asserted obscurantism of the Church with regard to the status of women. At Saülengasse there was much to make such rhetoric seem plausible.

The attachment of the pleasure-loving Schubert to the gloomy, severe, intolerant Mayrhofer, whose character was in some ways similar to the Schoolmaster's, is thus explicable. The verse which the latter supplied to Schubert in itself offers no very secure hold for Franz's imagination. It is never precise or concrete enough for Schubert's pictorial imagination. Again and again, as in *Sehnsucht* (Opus 8), the poet displays a scene of vivid imagery exciting to the composer's mind, only to snatch it away from him in the next stanza with some stagnant maundering about death and inclusive coming-to-naught.

The torment of melancholia and intellectual masturbation which Mayrhofer's writings reveal suggest some tragedy of frustration embedded in the very fibre of his being. The tragic element was there. Mayrhofer was a revolutionary, and as a vigilance officer of the censorship he was engaged, for the sake of a wretched living, in the suppression of his faith, a faith which was all the more disturbing for being obscure. His life was not wholly dissimilar from Schubert's. At first vivacious and acutely intelligent, *his* father intended him for the Church, to which end he was placed in a seminary, where he first distinguished himself by acquiring a sound knowledge of Greek and then by totally rebelling against such a career. He entered the tobacco trade ; next he read a pamphlet against the loathly plant and abjured sin, recanted, and sensibly proceeded to make amends by consuming enormous bulks of tobacco for the rest of his life.

At first, despite a squalid poverty which for a while Franz made radiant by sharing it with him, happiness possessed him. Then, little by little, a permanent blackness shut out every gleaming thing. His art, mainly concerned with classical myth, made a decrepit bridge into a better world. When it collapsed he fell into the Styx, as once he flung himself into the Danube upon hearing of the fall of Warsaw during the attempted Polish revolution.

After Schubert's death fate made a melancholy Petrouchka of Mayrhofer. He became aware of the Germ, awareness became terror, which in typhus-swept Vienna was fatal, though Death cheated his million servants with a macabre jest. One day when Mayrhofer went to a friend's house to play cards, a young doctor reported that cholera had also broken out. The melancholy poet was so horrified that he refused a glass of beer because of the germs it might contain. Next morning, being told of the death of a colleague's child, he flung himself from a third-storey window. Having by then lost all fear of the Germ, he received the sacrament in the street and died on the way to hospital.

Another revolutionary member of the Schubert circle was Senn, a turbulent young poet who, after a term of imprisonment, was banished to his native province. He was especially beloved by Schubert, who once sympathetically deplored his violence and added that he himself could never follow that road. Bauernfeld, one of the most notable of the group, was of like mind. The libretto of the *Count of Gleichen*, which he wrote for Schubert's last operatic venture, was actually forbidden by the censorship, stubbornly ignoring which Franz continued to work upon the music.

The composition of a funeral march upon the death of Alexander I of the Russias has puzzled some biographers, aware of how little Schubert was enamoured of the aristocracy and how incapable of imposing his will upon them. (The verb is Beethoven's.)

Alexander I was the liberal Czar, unjustly credited with reforming zeal, and until Metternich won him over, engaged in heavily subsidising the liberal secret societies throughout Europe, particularly in Austrian Italy. In one of Schubert's letters there is an odd reference to his painter-friend Kupelwieser, then in Italy. Kupelwieser was getting on well but was dissatisfied with his Russian. The chatter of the political groups can faintly be overheard in that strange dedication of music to an alien monarch.

Schubert had fled from a family whose design and spirit were copies of the State. This radical ambience suggests that he recognised in the ideals of his friends a like protest. It is consistent with expectation that he never attempted to express these views in action. For him music was the one valid protest. Probably without his being aware of it, his

most characteristic work of these early years,
the songs, were themselves a denial of the
courtly manners and taste. Their simple,
unsophisticated Germanic lyricism was in
strongest contrast with the Italianate tyranny
of courtly music. The relationships of Roman-
ticism to the liberal resurgence of the preceding
era are not obscure to literary scholars.
Schubert was in his songs the greatest of
Romantic musicians ; it is natural therefore
that the whole drive of his genius should have
impelled him away from the formalism and
sterile discipline of orthodox social conceptions.

In the folk-like directness of the songs
Schubert was returning to the people for
inspiration, as had Weber in *Der Freischütz*,
and his Viennese predecessors in the renais-
sance of German song, Steffan, Rupprecht,
Holzer and Grünwald, to mention no more.
The same tendency can be observed in the
ländler and the waltzes, this latter being a
dance which was prohibited at the Vienna
Congress balls when Franz II was present,
as being too undignified for a monarch. It
was the year of liberation, 1817, which saw
the appearance of this popular strain in the
severest of forms, the E♭ sonata being full
of it.

So, too, the richness of nature music in the songs has attracted all men's notice. It is hardly coincidence that Rousseau was the rediscoverer of both Nature and liberalism.

Had he been content to continue composing the largely conventional quartets and symphonies of his childhood, as many at that day were content, the Saülengasse quartet and orchestra would have been a satisfying comfort for poverty. The point will be later argued in terms of musical analysis, but it is now evident that the man and his music were one. Mozart, whose aristocratic temperament did not find a courtier's life too irksome despite the basest indignities, conquered the Italian opposition by a glorious compromise of which *Figaro* is the type. The imperious Beethoven repulsed it utterly on its last battle-ground with the democratic nobility of *Fidelio*. Each master clear-sightedly evolved his forms. The problem of why Schubert was so late in securing control of the forms necessary to his new material can be approached by the biographer. With large but easily discoverable elisions the argument lies embedded here ; Schubert possessed the qualities neither of heroism nor compromise.

57

VII

It was in this first year of freedom that Schubert met Vogl, the singer who was to do so much for the composer's contemporary fame. It was Schober who persuaded the massive and imposing Vogl to meet Franz. 'Not so bad,' he said at the interview, after examining the *Erlking*. 'There's good stuff in you but you are too little of an actor and not enough of a charlatan. You are wasting your ideas instead of developing them.' He may have wanted a few trills in the *Erlking's* entreaties, but this was nevertheless a great admission from one of the leading opera singers of his day. For parallel one has to imagine some penniless and unknown bohemian in Pimlico being first praised and then taken up by Signor ——, who recently declared it humiliating to be offered a nightly fee less than £350, a sum equal to about two-thirds of Schubert's life earnings. Vogl became Schubert's champion, a little oppressively, but always with love and veneration. His first remark to Schubert sprang from the wisdom of experience. He was a good man, a genuine scholar with a considerable knowledge of Greek, which he chose to read in the wings between calls.

How Schubert lived in 1817 is unknown. He had no income, and it must be believed that his friends, Schober, Spaun, Hütten-brenner and others, maintained him. After a while his father softened his heart too and made him loans, which were always scrupulously repaid, if with long delay. Poverty could not repress his spirits ; his prevailing humour is to be seen in the dedication of one song ' To Mr. Schober's apartment.' There were fewer compositions in 1817 ; forty-seven songs accompanied a quantity of transitional instrumental work, chief of which are the B Major, E♭ Major and A Minor piano-forte sonatas and the two quartets, numbers 10 and 11.

A musical friend introduced Schubert to Count Esterhazy, who offered him a post in his household upon generous terms. He was to be given board and lodging during the summer at the Count's country residence at Zelécz in Hungary, and in addition he was to receive two gulden for every lesson given to

the three children. In winter, when Esterhazy was following the court season in Vienna,
he would pay for lessons only. Schubert
accepted and duly accompanied the Ester-
hazys to Zelécz, where he was quartered in
the bailiff's lodge.

The justificatory function of the pyramidal
order of society, explains Dean Inge, is to
sustain at its apex an aristocratic strata which
by its refinement and wealth shall encourage
artists who create beauty at two gulden a
time. A less reputable purveyor of a more
material beauty than Schubert's would have
rejected the fee and not have shrunk at a
frank description of the proposed transaction.

But there is no need to waste compassion on
Franz. Zelécz did not stimulate many compositions, but it did not burden his soul greatly.
He wrote lightheartedly to his brothers and
friends, longing to be back in the beloved city.
He heartily enjoyed the country, and better
even than the later rhapsodies from Upper
Austria are his observations on the manner of
farming.

' The corn is not gathered into barns as
in Austria, but stacked in the fields in what
are called Tristen. These are often 80 to

100 yards long and 50-60 feet high, and they are built so nicely that the rain runs off them without doing any damage.'

The musical imagist of the songs might have been writing to his peasant grandfather.

Later he wrote to Schobert—the fusion of their names is revealing—a delightful description of his associates. He concludes, ' So far I have been spared an invitation to the dining-room.' He took his meals with the servants, in the company of the butler, who was his rival for the favours of a pretty chambermaid. There were plenty of occasions for music at Zelécz, and the sojourn also strengthened the popular element in his art by providing him with good Hungarian tunes and colouring.

It was there that the astonishing Count Stefan episode occurred. Stefan was a cousin of Esterhazy and a half-maniac musical dilettante, whose fantastic scrawls were placed before Schubert for interpretation, at his employer's command. This was not difficult, for while Count Stefan imagined himself Beethoven's equal as a composer, he could not read music.

Upon one such occasion Franz began to improvise a preludial passage of little lyrical melodies which eventually lead to a breakneck and colourful allegro con fuoco, probably upon the suggestion of the bedlam manuscript, the leaves of which he was carefully turning. Soon the music became so exciting that Schubert forgot all such pretence and continued to peal out his allegro, forgetful of Stefan sitting near. Suddenly a suspicion of the fraud penetrated the Count's intelligence, and he jumped up, eyes flashing with wrath. This brought Franz back to earth, and hastily suppressing the allegro he began to turn the pages again, with greater observance of probability, so that after a while Stefan grew calm and once more attentive to his own music.

When the improvisation was over, Schubert went up to the composer intending to confess, having already declared his intention of doing so to his friend Schlösser, who was present, saying that the deception weighed heavily upon his conscience. But once before Stefan, what Franz did was to advance the most ingenious excuse that a particular passage in the Count's Fantasia had led him away by its impetus. 'Why should a composer be more guilty than a poet who warms his own intellect with the flames of others? More than that I did not do.' Extemporising thus, Schubert broke into a passionate elaboration of the argument, with such seriousness that everyone was hard pressed to refrain from open laughter.

The incident tells us more about Franz than Stefan. It is believable that he meant to confess until the very moment when he looked into the face of the unfortunate man, and that he perceived at once that in their respective orders the splendid improvisation and the melancholy scrawl were one music.

Upon his arrival in Vienna during November, Schubert, who had obtained a year's leave, without the thirty-two shillings, was ordered by his father to return to the school. He refused, whereupon the Schoolmaster, in a furious access of paternality, again forbade him the house. But the City was there to receive him, there were irresponsible friends from whom rigour was as remote as the minor literature of the Samoyedes, and the huge liberty of blank staves waiting to be filled. For two years Franz lived with Mayrhofer in a bohemian communism of clothes, tobacco and books, occupying a wretched room with a superannuated piano, a few decrepit sticks and a guitar, rented from a French widow with the nice name of Sanssouci. Even the noble gloom of the poet could not withstand

the radiance of that friendship. He indulged
in solemn horseplay, often rushing at his room-
mate with a sword-stick and classic yells, to
be met with romantic defiance in broad
Viennese dialect.

The first weeks of 1819 saw the composition
of an opera, *The Twins*, to a most misbegotten
text by Hoffmann out of a Frenchman's muse.
Vogl, who sponsored it, doubled the leading
parts upon its performance at the Kärntnerthor
theatre. Nothing could have carried off the
impossible story, and the Twins died at the
end of a week. There was a contested first-
night call for the composer, but abashed by
his disreputable clothing and rejecting the
loan of the dress coat which Anselm Hüttenbrenner hastily stripped off, he refused to
appear, and Vogl was forced to announce
that Schubert was not in the theatre.

A good deal of unfinished work dates from
this period : a fine C Minor movement for
string quartet, an opera, *Sakuntala*, upon an
even more abominable libretto, are examples.
But if distraction was in part the cause of it,
yet it was not wholly ; Schubert's growing
maturity may at times have caused him uncertainty. Nor was the creative lull necessarily undesirable, it may have given him time

to reflect. Beethoven's mighty emergence from his silent years will be remembered. Such a song as the great *Prometheus* is evidence of growth.

The routine of Franz's daily life was now much as it was to be for the rest of his life. Having slept without troubling to remove his steel spectacles, he would rise and sit down to compose, often without completing his dressing. Reports are unanimous concerning his appearance during these morning hours. He was transfigured by the excitement of composition, his face, ordinarily a little puffy and dark-skinned, with low forehead and small eyes, became illuminated and vivacious, his bearing and manner were completely changed, even his voice. His composition was always done at a table and never within reach of the piano, and, in the early years at any rate, to finish one was to begin another. The afternoons were spent as fancy dictated, at music or in walking in the neighbourhood of Vienna or Währing, drinking beer at the Black Cat or the Snail near St. Peter's church, or if anyone had money, wine. Evenings brought the reunion of the Circle, now grown considerably, at a Gasthaus or tavern, often ending with a round of the coffee-houses, horse-

play, bell-pulling and such like amusements.
More responsible circles became open to him,
notably the musical parties of the four Frölich
sisters, enthusiastic and gifted musicians, who
lived honourably but without timidity or con-
vention. Kathi, the youngest and most beautiful, was at one time engaged to one of Schubert's
poets, the erratic Grillparzer, whose principal
difficulty was that he wanted all four of the
sisters. He broke with Kathi, returned headlong to the wretched but loyal girl, alternately
wooed and trifled with her for a number of
years, and then for the rest of a neurotic life
of high poetry and low spirits maintained a
profound friendship with her which unjustly
earned her the reputation of being his mistress.
Nothing so simple was possible for the complicated Grillparzer, but Viennese moralists, as
others, were convinced of the inevitability of
evil. Kathi Frölich exercised a great and
wholesome influence over Franz, not hesitat-
ing to rebuke his excessive living. The famous
Schubertiaden now began, gatherings of en-
thusiasts who united to perform and hear the
songs which delighted them and which Vogl
frequently sang to Hüttenbrenner's accompaniment, Schubert himself often singing or
extemporising at the piano. It was one of

these new acquaintances, Sonnleithner, who organised a subscription edition of a group of songs, among which was the *Erlking*, the first to be published, and by the editorial thug Diabelli, who had already turned them down as a business venture. *Der Wanderer* is said to have made him 27,000 florins in the course of a few years.

It is doubtful whether Schubert ever met Beethoven at this period. The untrustworthy Schindler says that Franz brought to Beethoven's house the four-handed Variations which he had dedicated to him, and upon admission was so dumbfounded at a kindly criticism that he fled the house. Hüttenbrenner, who accompanied Franz on this visit, explicitly denies this account. Beethoven was absent, and the Variations were left with a servant. Schubert had repeatedly seen Beethoven at the tavern which he frequented, and heard him damning the French and extolling the English, but his reverence was too great for the effrontery of self-presentation.

But above all, it was the night-life of the tavern which became the predominating influence in Schubert's life. It was now that he became a 'shadow' or novice in the bohemian society of intellectuals known as

Ludlam's Cave, founded by the dramatist and musical critic Castelli in 1810.

Ludlam's Cave first met at the Flying Horse, whence it removed to The Little Flowering Plant, upon inquiries by the Viennese Yard (Political Section), which suspected it of being subsidised by Russia. It embraced the cream of intellectual Vienna, and its conduct would have delighted Lewis Carroll. Every member received a Cave name, usually a derisive hit at some personal characteristic. Keyboard of the Calf's Foot hides the identity of the dignified pianist Moscheles, who had a passion for that dish. Grillparzer was the Istrian Sapphocles, so named because of a classical drama on the poetess. Bergreen, a minister at the British Legation in Constantinople, was known as Argantir, Abdullah of Ararat ; Discantino of the Beerpot was a university beadle who sang well under drink, Griffin of the Ratgut denoted the 'cello virtuoso Hauschka upon whom Beethoven invoked the blessing of open bowels when that gentleman approached him for a composition on behalf of the Society of Music Friends. Sedlatscheck, the flute-player, was called plain Sedl in summer and plain Latscheck in winter. Don Lemnos Santos y Templos and Cinnamon Twig of the South, this latter an artist who toured a peep-show, were popular members, and since names of all nationalities had to be employed, the disguise of one Ting tang ping pung pang probably perplexed the police with visions of the Yellow Peril.

Its Grand Caliph was the huge vermilion-faced court actor Schwartz, chosen for his thick-headedness and the possession of a daughter, and who died babbling of Ludlam after its final suppression. The Cave was a long unventilated room upon the first floor, where the night was spent in table-thumping art debates, piquant story-telling, singing, buffoonery and all manner of agreeable levity, including the large consumption of the good drink for which The Little Flowering Plant was famous. A deaf and dumb language was invented by Castelli, who imposed fines for bad grammar in its use. Ludlam being rich in musicians—Schubert, Carl Maria von Weber, Moscheles, Carl Blum, the Englishman Julius Benedict, were all associates—a mock opera was produced. One of Castelli's favourite pieces of nonsense appears to have been to put boots on his hands, dress himself in a long cloak beneath which an accomplice was concealed, and standing at a table, to deliver a mock oration while the accomplice made gestures with his hands. This can be so funny as almost to cause a great embarrassment, as I know who have seen it performed by a canon of the cathedral chapter of Vich and a priest of Berga after dinner when the wine had flowed.

It was this Castelli who provided the best libretto Schubert ever received. Its original title was *The Conspirators*, but the Censor objected to this as seditious. Since Karl Marx had not then written, they were permitted to call it *The Household War*. The music is light and cheerful, though there is no attempt at characterisation. At the first performance, long after Schubert's death, Castelli, then an old man, explained his neglect of the work by saying that he was told that Schubert's music was invariably gloomy. Nothing gloomy could have come out of Ludlam's Cave, as its founder should have known ; even its suppression was hilarious. The police, interpreting its high spirits as perforce a conspiracy against the cheerless Hapsburgs, raided The Little Plant and plucked all its blooms. After their farcical trial and acquittal the police chief, in order to turn a deaf ear to public derision, dived headlong from a window and extravagantly broke his neck.

High spirits and congenial living put down poverty, a poverty which was often, though not always, the result of indiscretion. In 1820 his opera *Zauberharfe* was produced at the An-der-Wien Theatre, but before Franz could receive a penny of his fee of 500 florins the management went bankrupt. The proceeds of Sonnleithner's effort had paid all Schubert's debts and left him a substantial sum, which soon disappeared the way long since heartily celebrated by Master Villon in his Ballade of Good Doctrine. Around the friendship-loving Franz were plenty of tavern-wits whose brilliance became even more comforting after wine. Nor is there any reason to shirk the other observations of Villon's great bottle-rattler. Already in the spring of 1821 Mayrhofer and the composer had parted, not by reason of enmity, but probably because the poet's unbroken severity ill-accorded with Franz's lighthearted ways. Schober was a more convivial friend. Schubert became subject to recurring fits of depression and religiosity, which suggest offences against conscience or discretion. The grimness of Saülengasse was far behind, the bonhomie and glamour of the city tavern had welcomed the youth yearning for warmth and understanding. But amid the glitter and cheer were temptations to pleasures the enjoyment of which at least requires a practical caution which the unprepared Schubert had not.

Towards the end of 1822 a violent illness manifested itself. Or rather, Schubert became exemplary to mankind, for whose benefit certain malignant ailments have been devised in order to turn him from frivolity and sin towards purer things, such as contemplation of the divine justice, the beauty of nature, or music.

Schubert had contracted venereal disease.

VIII

Distressing as the subject may be, it is necessary to consider what the effects of this malady may have been.

The disease became so virulent during the opening days of 1823 that Schubert was compelled to enter the Viennese General Hospital, where he was placed under a regime of baths, medicines and diet, and in every way given the best treatment available. In this predicament he received the comfort of his friends, for though authentic information was not then to be obtained in copies of a special leaflet, prudery had not yet been discovered as an aid to salvation and the best parlours. Kupelwieser's fiancée kept in repair the wig which he wore throughout a whole year, a severe rash having robbed him of his hair.

A powerful constitution, inherited from a long line of peasant ancestors, resisted well the disease, but from now until his death Franz was subject to recurrent outbreaks, often provoked by his own neglect. In February 1824 he had so far recovered that he discontinued the medicines. The malady immediately prostrated him, and he was ordered to fast for a fortnight, which he did.

A word of warning is necessary. Nothing in these conjectures as to the effect of Schubert's illness must be held to justify such theories as are contained, for instance, in Lange-Eichbaum's ' Problem of Genius.' We are concerned only with the *urge* to creation and the direction it took in a man of genius, not with the *possession* of creative genius, much less its inner analysis, which must always defy understanding. This remark is needed only because the miserable theory that vital disorder is essential to genius has derived some support from the lives of musicians, including Schubert. Such appeals are always made with a disgusting ignorance of the materials. And this warning must be held to apply to such analyses of character as I have presented in this book. Schubert undoubtedly reacted from the rigours of family and State, it is the duty of the biographer to make this clear, but this is still no explanation of genius.

It was natural that such a predicament as Schubert now found himself in should unsettle his hitherto almost unbroken good-humour.

In part we have indisputable data. At times black depression descended upon him from which he emerged with cheer but less of natural buoyancy. Upon the 31st of March 1824 he wrote to Kupelwieser in Rome :

' At last I can pour out my whole heart to someone again. You are so good and faithful, you are sure to forgive me things that others would only take very much amiss. To be brief, I feel myself to be the most unfortunate and miserable man in the world. Picture to yourself someone whose health is permanently injured and who, from stark despair, does everything to worsen it rather than improve it. Picture to yourself . . . someone whose creative inspiration for all that is beautiful is like to fail. . . . So I pass my days joyless and friendless, except when Schwind comes now and again to see me and brings with him a gleam of light from the sweet days that are gone.'

It is only fair to say that the fraudulent failure of Barbaja, manager of the Kärntner-thor theatre, to produce or pay for the commissioned opera *Fierabras*, had also dejected him.

Next day he records a forceless attempt to

recapture religious faith. ' Man comes into the world with faith, which is far superior to knowledge and understanding, for in order to understand a thing one must first of all believe in it. Reason is nothing more than analysed belief.' Too often it is unanalysed belief, but again it sounds like the memory of a lecture ; the thought occurs in St. Augustine.

There is also an invocation to Imagination. ' O remain with us, though venerated only by a few, so that we may be protected from so-called enlightenment, that hideous skeleton, without blood or flesh.' There is a common species of tavern talk which first identifies enlightenment with the rejection of tyrannous scruples, this with amorality and then by a deft change of prefix, arrives full-flush in the liberty which franker minds achieve with much less pother.

Nor did Schubert accomplish any serious reform in his ways ; through Kathi Frölich we hear of him becoming so tipsy at a friend's musical party that he had to be carried into another room. He did not visit the Frölichs between 1823 and 1824. To confront Kathi was too much for his delicate sensibility.

Wilhelm von Chezy, who met Schubert somewhat later, describes him thus :

'The little stocky musician, apparently a lump of fat but with glittering eyes that revealed at once the inner fire . . . took, shall I say, a certain pride in the accidents which befell him in his wild ways. When intoxicated he did not rant but moved into a corner to give himself up to a quiet frenzy. A smiling tyrant who . . . would destroy something, glasses, plates or cups.'

Von Chezy's truthfulness has been questioned, principally because he was a son of the authoress of *Rosamunde* and *Euryanthe*. The poetess was, according to Weber, an agreeable writer but an insufferable woman. The lady also did not wash frequently, but this by oversight has not been advanced against Wilhelm. Anselm Hüttenbrenner says of Franz that he was 'absolutely true, honest and upright,' and adds that 'at that time, between you and me, he lived a much purer life than I did.' There are, of course, degrees in the matter, as La Vie Parisienne insists.

It has often been remarked that Schubert's poverty was partly the result of his ineffectual dealings with publishers. There is no data before 1822, but this weakness became more pronounced as time went on. The magnificent

Winterreise only brought him 10d. apiece in 1828.

Now one of the effects of Franz's malady is, in an honest man such as he was, to prevent marriage. He might never have married, though most of his circle did, but as marriage or other healthy sex experience is one of the strongest incentives in life, this may in some measure explain his weakening of character. The hypothesis receives support from the music of the period. On the 27th of March 1824 he wrote :

> ' All that I have created is born of my understanding of music and my own sorrow. That which is born of grief alone seems to please the world least of all.'

This cannot simply mean that he expresses his sorrow in music, for in the second sentence he speaks of ' grief alone ' which would thus mean an inaudible music. He means to limit the place of personal sorrow in art, his sense is ' born of my sorrow and of my understanding of what music ought to be.' Now what music of his had recently displeased the world ? Schober gives the information. The *Schöne Müllerin* itself had recently failed with the public. Schober was furious about it and seems crazily to have suggested that Schubert should bribe the critics. (Schubert had no money.) The song cycle had been begun while Schubert was in hospital in 1823. Their author was not a miller, despite the taunt of Convict days, but like the young journeyman of the songs, he had set out with joy, to find despair and destruction. There is said to be little irony in Schubert, but those who hear the *Schöne Müllerin* with the composer's life in mind will experience irony.

Irony is of divers sorts. Of the subtle tincturing of every chord with acid flavour, and similar gallicisms, there is little in his music. But of the more elemental method of placing conflicting emotions in continuity there is plenty. The first method has the merit of enabling a fine craftsman to amuse sophisticated audiences, the second has the demerit of requiring a musical genius for its bringing-off. What would have happened with a sincere second-rater is that either his *Wohin* would have lacked the buoyancy of youth or his *Die Liebe Farbe* and *Trockne Blumen* would have been mere turgidities. The ghastly irony is that in writing that clear rippling water-music of *Wohin* the man lay upon his bed with a fiery anguish in his loins. The whole cycle is a magnificent tribute to the unifying power of irony. The poems had ensured that the brook should be the text of the irony, but that *Wohin* is so utterly carefree nothing but genius could have ensured. A powerful sense of irony working through a mind of technical facility is able to evoke for its purpose the very image of an emotion for lack of which the spirit weeps in despair. All the more so because this experience of joy is temporary and must in a while be shattered, all within the limit of a handful of songs. It may not have been merely chance that these poems of love frustration appealed to Franz so powerfully. At that time he bore in him that which barred out love from his own life.

There is one song of 1823 which also excites the imagination, *Der Zwerg*. The absurd poem tells the story of a dwarf court jester who became enamoured of a queen and therefore, enjoyment of her being impossible, he strangled her.

We happen to know how this song was composed. One day Randhartinger called upon Franz and invited him to take a walk. He consented, but asked for a few minutes in which to compose a song, which was thereupon written out at lightning speed, while the friends continued to laugh and jest with one another. These are the very conditions when one might fairly expect the subconscious to come to the aid of the artist. It is precisely this song which astonishes the critics, who see in it a promise of what Schubert might have done in opera had he met the right libretto. They should have said the right story.

To play over the pianoforte part alone is indeed to be amazed. The threatening gloom of the theme in the bass is tremendously impressive. It matters nothing that Schubert makes use of the ' fate motive ' of Beethoven's Fifth Symphony, of which he was a great admirer ; the *Erlking* itself draws on *Fidelio*. What matters is the dark and brooding significance of the music, as tragic as Wagner and far more economical.

It is agreed that upon his second visit to Zelécz in 1824 Franz fell in love with Caroline Esterhazy. But as he had been teaching her during the preceding winter it would be strange if this affection did not pre-date that year.

Caroline Esterhazy might as well have been a queen. Her exalted rank would have made unthinkable any union with a mere musician

F   81

who, while he was not a dwarf, suffered an equivalent physical disability, and one most intimately connected with the most powerful of subconscious forces. Such a disability would even have enabled him to become enamoured of Caroline, for just as certain youths only behave amorously towards married women, who cannot put them to the test of marriage, Schubert may instinctively have chosen a woman whose unapproachable rank forbade passionate response. If this were so this compensation for lost love would almost certainly be effective, especially if Caroline smiled upon him, knowing of his love. She did know, and one day asked him why he dedicated none of his compositions to her. His immediate reply was that all of them were already so dedicated. Moreover, Franz possessed a miniature portrait of her which it is difficult to believe could have been obtained without her consent.

Whereas the first Zelécz visit had been comparatively sterile, the second one produced the ' Divertissement à l'hongroise,' the four-handed pianoforte sonata in B♭ and the Opus 140 in C, vast and noble as a symphony, which it almost certainly was intended to be and which it eventually became

in Joachim's scoring. After 1824 Franz did
not again visit Zelécz.

Violence crept into his temper, though displays of it were rare unless drink had already
roused him. In February 1823, in the very
moment of distress, he had sold the entire
rights of his published works to the tempter
Diabelli, who never made a paltry grant to
the ailing and nearly destitute man, despite a
fortune reaped from the works. Schubert has
been criticised for the improvident sale, but
his need of immediate money can be well
imagined. In April he wrote a stinging letter
to Diabelli, saying bluntly that he had become
aware of his dishonest intentions. He had
overcharged Schubert for the copying of his
opera by fifty florins and deducted it from
his royalties. He complained that the firm
had not delivered his complimentary copies
and suspects that sales returns have been
falsified.

One night after the New Wine Festival at
Grinzing the Circle had finished up at a
favourite tavern. Schubert, slightly drunk and
very excited, began to discourse acutely of
music, during which a party of professional
musicians entered. After flattery they tried
to wheedle a composition out of Franz, who

at once commendably drank up his punch and let loose a hurricane of very able abuse.

'One of you bites into the mouthpiece of a wooden cudgel and the other blows himself out on a French horn. Is that Art? *I'm* an artist, not only a composer of country dances as the stupid Daily Mails and Daily Expresses say (free translation) and idiots repeat.' After another bout of lustiness of this sort Franz's temper took a higher flight. 'Creeping and gnawing worms that my foot should crush! The foot of a man who reaches to the stars! *Sublimi feriam sidera vertice !* Translate that for them,' he added in a prudent aside, and then as the flummoxed hacks had nothing to say, sat down and ordered more punch. In the early hours of the morning they got him home, where he flung his clothes about the room, and before getting into bed with his spectacles on wrote the aphorism, 'Oh Enviable Nero! Thou who wast strong enough to destroy a corrupt people with the sound of stringed instruments and with song !' But for all that he rose with a laugh next morning, saying to the reproving Bauernfeld that he would probably write the soli, after which the players would kiss his hands.

Such indiscretions may have been the result

of bohemian high spirits, but it is conceivable that his improvident living was not unconnected with the despair induced by his malady. The necessities of chronological biography alone prohibit development of the theme.

IX

1823 deepened Schubert's love for the painter
Moritz von Schwind, and the fine spiritual
face of the portrait of that year explains this
well enough.   Joseph Hüttenbrenner also
served the composer devotedly, retrieving lost
manuscripts and interviewing publishers, besides making vain efforts to secure production
of his friend's operas.

The following year, Schober having with
some secrecy departed on a disastrous theatri-
cal tour in North Germany, Franz took a
room next to the Moonshine House, Schwind's
home, in order to be near his friend, about
whom he used somewhat extravagant expressions, calling him ' My Beloved.'   Schubert
was again on good terms with the Schoolmaster, who advanced the rent of his apartment during a destitute period.   With Schwind,
and Bauernfeld a little later, Franz began to
repeat the communal life he had practised
with Mayrhofer.   Schwind's studio was the
Citadel, often besieged by Dwarfs, from whom

the persecuted ones fled, over the garden wall, rather than be confronted with tailor's and bootmaker's bills. Gold Dust was common property, and one day, a pipe to smoke it in being missing, one was contrived out of Schubert's spectacle case. This cheerful tom-foolery, accompanied by high music-making, poetry-writing and painting is the obverse of the gloom described, and it was certainly more abiding than that gloom. It was at the Moonshine House that Schubert met the del Rio family, with the intelligent daughters of which Beethoven had once discussed free love.

Schubert was more prosperous in 1825, the peak year of his first artistic maturity. He received £20 for the Lady of the Lake songs, and appeared to Bauernfeld, afterwards to achieve fame as a dramatist, as a veritable Croesus. With Vogl he toured Upper Austria in the summer, triumphing everywhere to his great joy. There is a touching anecdote of the composer applying leeches to the invalid son of Traweger, his landlord at Gmunden, when the child would not permit the approach of the doctor. The boy conceived a great love for Schubert and often crept into his bed in the early morning. Attempts to repeat this with the lordly Vogl were met with prompt ejection, however. He wrote a long and very proper letter to his parents from Steyr, recounting the success of his songs, in particular the Hymn to the Virgin, adding, ' There was great surprise at my piety too . . . I never compose hymns or prayers of this sort unless I am involuntarily overcome by a sense of devotion, and then the feeling is, as a rule, genuine and heartfelt.'

In a much longer letter to Ferdinand he gives an ecstatic description of the gorgeous scenery around Steyr. The letter is true to the character of the song-writer, he does not lose himself in vague descriptions of the mountains, but notices how in the villages around Salzburg the wooden kitchen utensils rest on wooden stands and these are placed outside the houses. A great Spanish realist, Pio Baroja, passing through Madrigal de la Vera, did not observe the same custom in that sun-dazzled village of the great Central Sierra. Schubert notes without regret certain inscriptions bearing witness to the vanished power of the Church, and in one place comments ironically upon the contrast between the squalor of the villages and the splendour of the great green hills. The Castle of Monat Schlössen which, he says, was built in one

month by a prince for his pretty lady, draws
from him the exclamation, ' Everyone knows
of this, but no one is shocked. What enchant-
ing tolerance ! ' But that the mountains
stirred the deep mysticism in him we know
from the glorious *Die Alemacht* written at
Gastein.

Upon his return to Vienna in October,
Schober was awaiting him, and the night-life
of Vienna promptly reclaimed the pair. That
winter Franz suffered a fresh outbreak of his
disease. There were new disappointments
also. Anna Milder, the German prima donna,
had been unable to secure a performance
of *Alfonso und Estrella*, Schubert's opera to
Mayrhofer's libretto. He had already forfeited
Weber's promised aid by his criticism of
Euryanthe.

An incident of this year reveals the generosity
of the man. A manuscript of Mozart's came
into his possession, and he and Anselm Hüttenbrenner played the work through together.
In order to commemorate the occasion Franz
offered to halve the manuscript with Anselm.
He declined to be responsible for dividing the
manuscript, whereupon Schubert proffered
him the whole. Hüttenbrenner accepted.

Ill fortune was once more attendant in 1826.

The dedication of Opus 40 to his friend and doctor, Bernhardt, discloses that he was again ill. In April he applied for the post of Assistant Kapellmeister at the court, but was unsuccessful. He mentions, among other things, that he had composed five masses, though if the emperor ever saw the application this was unfortunate. Franz II was pious, but he preferred short masses. The post of conductor at the Court theatre also became vacant, and his appointment to this was made to depend upon the successful writing of some numbers for the theatre. He did this, but the singer Schechner collapsed beneath the high notes and the battery of brass. Still more appeals from the most influential friends were brought to a sudden conclusion by Schubert, who slammed the score together, and with the words ' I shall alter nothing,' stalked out of the theatre.

The intrigue and indiscipline of operatic circles of that time restrain criticism. The Schubert who never misjudged an accompaniment and in whom there is no bad scoring was probably ill-served and aware of it. But such a gesture, effective enough in a successful and combative man, suggests that Franz was modelling his conduct on that of Beethoven.

Fees were declining, too. Nägeli of Zurich wrote asking for a pianoforte sonata, for which Franz requested a fee of less than £3. To this exorbitant demand the publisher disdained to reply. It would almost seem that the Continental trade possessed its secret service after the manner of armament manufacturers, and knew very well that sooner or later Schubert could be beaten down to a handful of pence for a major work. Probst also complained that Schubert's music was eccentric and incomprehensible, which must be a reflection on his engravers.

The Frölichs' house now became a haven in his distress, and he was often found in the sisters' company. The story of Schubert's final reconciliation with the Frölichs makes gracious reading. One day Kathi was sitting in the music-room when the door slowly opened a few inches, just sufficient for Franz to peer round, timidly blinking through his little spectacles. ' Miss Kathi, may I come in ? ' he asked, and upon being gently scolded for doubting her welcome, replied that he had been afraid to present himself because of her frown of disapproval at him one day when they had met in the street.

A visit to Gmunden was abandoned in this

year, through lack of money. Mayrhofer and Bauernfeld departed on subsidised tours, the former to survey for the tax collectors, the latter ostensibly as a member of his staff, but really to engage himself with the libretto of the *Count of Gleichen* which he had promised Schubert. It is curious that Mayrhofer did not point out the inadmissibility of the plot, but perhaps the Viennese censor was a quantity as uncertain as our own local, very local Lord Chancellor.

The *Death and the Maiden* quartet, though sketched earlier, and the great quartet in G (Opus 161) are the pinnacle achievements of 1826. Indeed with the first-mentioned quartet Schubert had reached the culminating point in the first stage of his maturity. It will be well, therefore, to suspend the narrative of his life for an examination of the music.

X

Upon 19th October 1814 Franz Schubert created German song with his *Gretchen am Spinnrade*, it has been said. There is little in the work of his predecessors to contest the judgment.

There is no space here to add one more to the lengthy commentaries on Gretchen, nor can words tell the tale of musical beauty. On the whole, critics have been most attracted by the accompaniment. There is in it every possible refinement, indeed. The perfect rhythmic mating of the treadle to the wheel, the rise in pitch as Gretchen treadles faster, and then, after her unrest has deepened into sorrow at the words ' und ach, sein kuss ' and the wheel has stopped, it begins falteringly and only with difficulty reaches its first tonality. All this is marvellous in a lad of seventeen, but it is not the most wonderful thing about Gretchen. It has an indefinable hallucinatory power, as if Schubert had actually seen *Faust* performed and had gone home to create the song, and hearing it, we ourselves seem not to be listening to a song, but to be remembering the drama. It is dramatic in the best sense, being ' a thing done.'

In 1815 came 144 songs, some of impossible length and showing a reversion to his earlier model, Zumsteeg. Most I like the strangely neglected *Das Geheimniss*, an almost ' fey ' expression of first love. The downward staccato figure in the left hand was to become a characteristic of Schubert. Of the Ossian songs five belong to 1815, but *Ossians Lied nach dem Falle* is alone worth attention. *Das Unendlichen*, of which there are three versions, and *Das Rosenband* are the best of the Klopstock songs of the autumn. Besides these minor poets Franz drew upon Goethe thirty times, and in a round dozen created enduring beauty. *Heidenröslein* is perhaps the most popular ; *Meeresstille*, so perfect in idea that no one can sing it ; *Erster Verlust* and the *Erlking* all show how the great poetry stirred Schubert most, a fitting answer to those critics who have charged him with poor taste in verse.

Gretchen and the *Erlking* are revelations of method, but *Mignon's Song*, written in October, tells us greatly about the urge to creation in Schubert. Beethoven, Schumann and Wolff

have all set this song, but none so well as
Schubert. The problem is to express both the
particular and the universal in this lovely
poem. That universal is the everlasting longing of the heart for a land in which the sun
shines perpetually, not only upon lemon
groves and the everlasting corn that shall
not be reaped of the Englishman Traherne,
but upon whatever crop the heart desire.
But this has to be done through the mouth
of a sad waif robbed out of Italy before the
years at which she could have loved her
country passionately. In doing it Wolf allowed
a burst of passion which is beyond his right ;
there is too much strength in Beethoven, and
though Schumann's is a fine effort, Schubert
alone knew the pathos of the girl's song. He
was a boy when he wrote it, and one whom
the Schoolmaster wished to rob out of his
own land.

The following year was much less fruitful,
the *Wanderer* being the most popular of its
productions. 1816 also saw some reversion to
Zumsteeg, but a notable group of Goethe songs
makes amends with the *Wiegenlied*, lovely
enough to be stolen, and *An Schwager Kronos*,
which might be translated ' To Buddy Time.'
The gaunt power of those pianoforte octaves

below the noble D Minor theme should thrill both performers, and towards the middle of the song, where the right hand grasps a line of marching chords and the left surges up out of the welter below, the music becomes utterly irresistible. *An die Laute* should be sung more often, it is a charming ländler-like serenade.

On the whole 1816 is a year of small songs, pure and colourful as Mediterranean islets, but set in a northern sea.

The year of Schubert's growing decision to leave home, 1817, produced only forty-seven songs, but these have increasing maturity, expressed in their greater flexibility and fullness of musical content. The awful *Gruppe aus dem Tartarus* and *Memnon* are the best examples of this legitimate straining of the medium. As a result of Mayrhofer's friendship, classical subjects are prominent, nearly always treated with the splendour they demand. The function of classicism in Mayrhofer's life is well seen in these songs. Here is nothing of Parnassean chill and restraint ; their passion indicates that they were an escape from an unlovable present. Schubert responded ; there can be nothing in music like the trumpeted irony of the closing pages of the *Tartarus*, the grandeur of the classic defiance of doom, which to our infinite harm supine pietism has almost obliterated, is simply magnificent. There is maturity too in *Der Tod und das Mädchen*, not the vaguest suggestion of the macabre disfigures it.

The flexibility of *Ganymed* and *Memnon* must be pointed out, and for honesty's sake the lovely falling passages upon the words ' All loving Father ' in the first-named. *Atys*, a young shepherd's lament for his lost home, is void of feeling, perhaps because the youth has been stolen away by the very willing lady Cybele. The searching melancholy of *Memnon* is surely subjective, but Mayrhofer's plea for Dawn to remove him to another and better place stirred Schubert to a glowing hymn to Light. Already the vibrating triplets begin to dazzle the inner eye with visions of the Schubert who might have been. This bears the stamp of Schubert's reaction to grief, which blazes out dazzlingly in the C Major Symphony of 1828, as if to step over the mere ditch of approaching death. That serenity, into whose white radiance the golden warmth of gratitude has been poured, glows once again in 1817, in the lovely *An die Musik* of the unworthy Schober ; and yet the pathos of the pianoforte phrase between the strophes hints almost too poignantly at the reason for gratitude.

Evidently one phase in Schubert's career as a song-writer is drawing to a close, for the year 1818 is distinguished by only fourteen songs. Only one of these has secured universal admiration, *Litanei*. Another, however, has provided a psychological problem of importance, the Mayrhofer *Einsamkeit*, with its seventeen pages of religious disillusionment, love, grief, commercial woe and all manner of rejection, ending in the peace of the forest and a cuckoo calling from green boughs. (Fortunately for the hero's peace the Shakespearian significance of the bird was not current.) ' I think it is the best thing I have done,' wrote Schubert, ' for my mind has been free from care.' This confidence was not justified, nor will the tale of his own life sustain his explanation. Apart from its length and abstraction, the poem was too naked an expression of that negativism at which Franz had magnificently baulked in *Memnon*. Though he fled to Nature again and again, he loved not solitude.

The Novalis hymns of next year are full of a rich grace-giving nature-mysticism rather than piety. Novalis also longed for death in his *Nachthymne*, and the French critic who has tried to prove that Schubert had a lifelong preoccupation with Death would do well to see how here he dismissed it with a perfunctory phrase. Mayrhofer's *An die Freunde* and *Sehnsucht* go to pieces for the same reason. Nothing could be more revealing than this constant failure of negativism to awaken great music in the most naturally musical of all geniuses. This man could support poverty with total indifference if only friendship and music remained, the deep sincerity of *An die Musik* had already told us that.

Two other Mayrhofer songs must be mentioned, the fine *Orest auf Tauris*, which instructs Orestes how he may avoid the parricide's curse, and *Der Entsühnte Orest*. The absolved Orestes stirs magnificent music in Franz.

The cold splendour of *Freiwilliges Versinken* almost foretells certain pages in Sibelius, as indeed does a good deal of Schubert. Here is proof that it is not only the greatest poetry which makes the finest music.

An 1820 song permits a perhaps fanciful comment ; *Der Zürnenden Diana* of Mayrhofer. The poet has been fatally wounded by the goddess, whom he has spied upon in her bathing pool. The price is not too great, he swears, and continues to gaze at the naked and vengeful beauty who, as St. Thomas Aquinas has enabled us to understand, preserved the accidents of woman while her substance was divine. Mayrhofer was only concerned with literature, like Shakespeare in 'Venus and Adonis,' as I once unavailingly explained to my form master, but surely the musician betrays a natural delight in his mental image in so flaming into music that he had to repeat the words again and again, not a common procedure with him. A Mayrhofer song of 1822, *Heliopolis* (*II*) is an invocation to the hearer to leave this world for a certain valley of crags and lakes, not there to die or to live the draughty life of a hermit, but because in that valley the passions may be freely and properly satisfied. An earnest psychologist looking for a doctorate might make a large thesis out of this theme, which may be called the ' Lost Island ' motif. From the Irish story of Brand to a modern Spanish poet this region of a lost age has been distinguished by one thing : delight in the flesh was not mortal to the soul there, ' And they lay under trees with beautiful women, without sin.' Schubert made of *Heliopolis* a splendid song. Wonderment has often been expressed that the great catholic mystics should have used the frankest of erotic imagery in describing their ecstasies; in the not unsensual Schubert one sees how a commonplace of erotic experience can soar as high as most hymns in the *Sei mir gegrüsst* of 1821, and reach heights undreamed of by most devotees in the later *Du bist die Ruh* of Rückert. The two phenomena are one and the same.

There is no space for more than mention of the charm of *Das Mädchen* and the calm solemnity of *Das Abendroth* ; the delightful *Die Sterne* and the amazing *Im Walde* must also be passed over, so too the grandeur of *Grenzen der Menscheit*. *Frühlingsglaube* provides occasion for an answer to Romain Rolland, who has objected to the innumerable *Frühlingsnachts, Frühlingsbotschafts* and *Frühlinglieder* of German song. The answer is, I suppose, that if one is lucky one spends a quarter of one's life in springtime, and with greater fortune still, the whole of it. The marvellous *Wanderers Nachtlied* of 1822 had the aid of a perfect poem upon an essential theme which Mayrhofer had too often turgidly bungled. Before this miracle of music nothing can be done to describe it. One hears it and perhaps, long after, the quaint literary thought occurs : what would the Chinese have done with song had they discovered the secret of music as they have that of the short poem ? *Auf dem Wasser zu singen* must be saluted and passed by in favour of the 1823 Leitner song, *Drang in die Ferne*. Here is a song of yearning for freedom which does not fail. Its happy, reckless spontaneity is all too rarely heard. Leitner did not propose an escape through death, but a youthful absconding over the wonders of the seven shining seas and the yellow cornfields and viridian plains of the coloured world, and Schubert, with his romantic sanity, agreed.

After *Die Schöne Müllerin* of 1823 Schubert for a while concerned himself with instrumental problems. 1824-1826 were the years of the great pianoforte sonatas and string quartets, in which he was searching for the perfection of expression long since acquired in the song. The prolific creativeness of youth has disappeared, but a power of artistry has been gained which without that earlier luxury could not have been achieved so young. The four Rückert songs of the autumn of 1823 in particular are the work of a mature mind.

Schubert still concerned himself with Mayrhofer's morbidities, and in *Der Sieg* he succeeded in grasping the pathos of the poem. Mayrhofer's gloom was deliberate and ineluctable, however. In *Abendstern* he asks the evening star why she is so lonely in the sky. The answer is that she is also Love and therefore solitary. Mayrhofer might at least have noticed that the evening star is rapidly followed by many others. Schubert did his best but failed ; nevertheless, the song is unjustly neglected.

The pinnacle of 1825 is *Die Junge Nonne*. Here is the perfection of musical poetry, proclaimed by its economy and subtlety. The nun, reflecting upon the lightning of mortal passion which once consumed her, is accompanied by the muttered theme which depicts the barely heard storm outside the convent. Yet no simple apposition is attempted, but rather the nun is made to reach ' a larger understanding of nature's way ' as the best of English critics of the songs has said. The Collin *Nacht und Traüme*, whose exacting beauty so often makes us uneasy in our seats lest the singer waver, also belongs to this year, as do the ' Lady of the Lake ' songs.

But now the grey moods of the oncoming *Winterreise* more and more invade Schubert's art. True, amongst *Ueber Wildemann* and *Tiefes Leid* and the almost bitter *Am mein Herz*, with its excess of despair, the delicious *Im Frühling* defies even the sorrow that the poet had mingled with its blue and green and gold.

The *Mignon* songs bring sadness again, and
just as the former loveliness had been from
within out of his own longing, these also were.
So lasst mich scheinen still has a grip on the world
which *Mignon* had not, and there is anguish
in the grip. *Im Freien* brings joy again, the
Wiegenlied tenderness, and a peculiar warmth
of gentle emotion makes *Silvia* justly popular;
but in retrospect the colours of 1827 are borne
down all of them by the noble gloom of the
Winterreise.

XI

NOTHING is more apparent to the earnest student of these songs than the robust sanity of their composer. Mayrhofer, it has been argued, provides the test, and again and again Schubert may be seen to evade his defeatism, by seizing upon an incidental beauty, by reinterpreting the poem or by simple failure of inspiration. We need no other explanation of the two men's separation in 1821.

But creation is nevertheless costly. I have suggested that Schubert matured in character under the stress of composition. The suggestion may seem unintelligible to some who think that experience alone achieves this ; but I think it must be granted that the most important experience in the life of a genius is that genius itself. Indeed, another explanation of Schubert's ineffectualness in life is that all his experience was of music. ' The greatest musician is he who knows only music,' says the Spanish proverb. Franz knew little else. Spaun, the most level-headed of Schubert's friends, declared that after he had completed the *Winterreise* Schubert was run down in health, even if not to an alarming point. . . . ' We who were near and dear to him knew how much the creatures of his mind took out of him. . . . No one who saw him at his morning's work . . . will ever forget it. I hold it beyond question that the excitement in which he composed his finest songs, the *Winterreise* in particular, brought about his untimely death.' Yet the most magnificent tribute ever paid to sanity by an artist (whose task in a farcical world this is) is this same *Winterreise*. The mood subtlety and the finesse of that last going off with the organ-grinder is superb. Here is the spiritual technique of Shakespeare's *Macbeth* porter again. The stroke was, of course, the poet's, but that the music did not fail in its task is wonder. Or by now it is no wonder there are no more failures in Schubert.

The most popular of comments on Schubert's songs is to draw attention to the delight in Nature which they evince. Instances are known to all. The cuckoo and the waterfall of *Einsamkeit*, the nightingale in *Ganymed*, the leaf, bird and brook of *Schlaflied*, the falling dew of *An den Mond in einer Herbstnacht*, the tossing boughs of *Nachthymne*, *Lindenbaum* and *Abendbildern*, and above all, the invariable success of his water music as in *Des Fischers Liebesglück*, *Auf dem Wasser*, *Das Lied im Grünen*, and the whole of *Schöne Müllerin*. So perfect is all this that I am sure that had Schubert met that perfect evocation of ' water running frizzled over gravel ' he would have found the means of its portrayal without hesitation.

Finer, however, in its sense of mystery and the cold hollow spaces of the sun-abandoned sky is *Freiwilliges Versinken*, the Novalis hymns, or subtler still, the integrated but not coincident rhythms of the *Wanderers Nachtlied*, which do far more than suggest the barely swaying boughs, but image the entire world's strife at rest, but only at rest, which is the heart-quelling beauty of Goethe's poem, not to be felt until one has absorbed the significance of ' Faust.'

Schubert's reaching of the universal through the vivid particular suggests that he almost belonged to that class of mind known as the eidetic, in which the mental image is so vivid as to become a percept, serving as a drop curtain to the world of normal experience. This eidetic intensity of vision and audition, we are told, is most apt to develop when there is retardation of discharge tendencies. If this eidetic quality was inherent in the man, certainly his life was such as to develop it to the full. The artist might almost be described as a flexible eidetic. The individuality of the songs after 1823 is amazing, each one seems to have been seen as an enacted ' thing ' of music. There is one song which more than any other calls for the richness of the orchestra, always a sign of the expanding genius of Schubert, *Der Doppelgänger*. If not Heine, at least one of Schubert's poets and the greatest, was eidetic. Goethe himself once witnessed that most terrible of all image-percepts, of the self, as when riding away from a tryst Goethe came face to face with Goethe riding back. Shelley also comes to mind, startling the household with shrieks of terror which he explained by saying : ' I have followed from my room the embodied shadowy image of myself.' It is impossible to hear *Der Doppelgänger* without an indescribable fear ; what that music might be like if through the bare harmonies of strings and bassoons a bass trombone surged softly, I do not know. That Schubert felt the immobile terror of that vision of himself standing before the house of long ago, even the pianoforte makes clear, without the voice whose very words of lost love recall the tragic city of *Die*

Stadt of the final year. ' The mist rising veils
the city. The breeze that wrinkles the water
is chill and the oars beat a mournful rhythm.
Ah, that last gleam of day. It shows up a
place where I lost love and all.' The brother-
hood in grimness of the two musics is to be
heard, but the intolerable farewell of *Die Stadt*
justifies the title of *Schwanengesang* which was
given without authority to the posthumous
songs.

It has been said that Schubert did not develop ; the opinion is incorrect. Name the
songs after 1827 ; the list is near to becoming
a record of successes. Nor is there any Schubert
pattern, each is utterly individual, yet of their
creator alone. The long Zumsteegean works
are left behind by 1819, the length of the
Schulze songs of 1825 being quite another
matter. The fusion of lyricism and declama-
tion which such songs as the *Atlas* exhibit are
a planetary remove from the simple alter-
natives of strophic song and *récitatif* with which
the early Schubert worked. The subtle deli-
cacy of such an unimportant song as Schober's
Nachtviolen is a league beyond the boy Franz,
for all the astonishing Gretchen. The ever-
deepening psychological insight, already matur-
ing in *Der Kampf* of 1817 is of even greater

artistic value to a song-writer than the visionary splendour of *Tartarus*, and leads to a fundamental point in the understanding of Schubert the man.

The opinion has been held that the tragic failure of the musician's life was what impelled him to seize upon such poems as those of the *Winterreise*. This has been disputed, and such songs as *Die Taubenpost* and *Die Sterne* have been advanced in support of the denial. But surely the problem has been clumsily misstated? Schubert himself gives us the clue. In that time of crisis in 1824 he wrote, 'Sorrow sharpens the understanding and strengthens the character.' It is his remarks upon understanding that are relevant. The consequence of travail upon a supremely great artist is not to cast him down into a ladderless pit of misery, but to deepen and darken the valleys and to make more glittering the peaks above them. And the genius walks in both ways and between. More and more this is what Schubert had learned to do. The first ripening had prematurely thrown off the Unfinished Symphony, the windfall of chance, as I think, in which the anguish and the joy are completely fused. The separated gloom and light of the later songs, the poignant shadow of the

Quintet in C of 1828, and the spiritual radiance of the C Major Symphony of that year, show that the immensity of our loss is rarely realised. Again there are huge elisions in the argument, but Schubert had only just begun to make the real music of his genius when death intervened.

XII

THERE is a Schubert problem in the music as in the life of the man. The incapacity to dominate, even to exact just treatment, is matched on the musical side by his asserted lack of form.

Schubert's instrumental music, in particular his essays in sonata form, it is said, are a treasury of thematic wealth from which, despite moments of exquisite poetry, a perfect work of art never emerges. The wisest and most generous of English scholars has made the criticism explicit in saying that Schubert's expositions digress into premature developments, his developments collapse into repetitious lyrical episodes, and that his recapitulations disclose the unsuitability of his expositions for that purpose. There must be no shirking of this problem, and the following three chapters devoted to the pianoforte music will therefore be concerned with the sonatas, rather than the popular short pieces.

There are three main time divisions in

Schubert's pianoforte composition in this form. The years 1815-1817, 1818-1825, 1826-1828 mark the limits of these periods, the terminal dates being in each case the peak year. With certain displacements the rhythm can be observed in Schubert's achievements in other mediums.

Two incomplete attempts date from 1815, the year of Franz's submission to the School-master. More important perhaps than an analysis of the first, in E Major, is its comparison with the abandoned draft of it made a few days earlier. This attempt had broken down, really because he had given out his second subject in the tonic key, and the natural result of the circulation of his material was that he would have been compelled to recapitulate his First Group in the dominant! Now, emphatically, these are not the errors of a well-taught student, but of one left to his own devices. For the rest, the most significant fact is that he deliberately begins his development in the key of F Major (the II ♭). From the outset he had evidently determined to explore tonality relationships to their limit.

An unfinished sonata in C Major of September clearly shows the influence of Beethoven. Schubert is seen delighting in Sturm und Drang and strong contrasts between his First and Second Groups. Incidentally, for reasons of Drang, the Second Group contains a member which somewhat strains the framework of the exposition. Much has been written about Mozart's influence over Schubert. From these two works it is almost entirely absent ; the menuettos, allegro vivace, are quite individual in their delight in clanging harmonic problems. It is the romantic impulse which is the most important matter in this attempt ; it does not take the form of lyricism, however, and is in this sense not really individual.

From 1815 until 1817 the home quartet and orchestra absorbed Schubert's efforts in sonata form, but in that year of his growing resolve to leave his profession the pianoforte again occupied him. An unfinished sonata in A♭ Major is especially interesting in the Mozartian sense of proportion which it discloses. A Beethovenish first movement in E Minor contains many personal elements such as the Left Hand (L.H. henceforth) triplets, and then follows the first completed sonata in B Major. Then in quick succession come the E♭ Major, known as Opus 122, an abandoned first movement, and Opus 164, Sonata in A Minor (note that Opus 42, the so-called first sonata, is a work of eight years later date).

The E♭ Major had originally been cast in D♭ Major, and in that key precedes the B Major Sonata by two months. The first striking fact about its opening movement is the abundant thematic material. Schubert has now formed his First Group out of strongly rhythmical and clearly defined elements of manageable size. This last is important, for it discloses that Schubert was thinking, thematically, in terms of the classical sonata. And most of his material was anything but classic in feeling. The Second Group, however, is enormous and very varied. The first member of the Second Group (2/1 : further indications will be given so) is an astonishingly vulgar tune of the false-popular type, similar to a Rossini clarinet tune. This idiom persists in Schubert but is rapidly refined ; it reappears, for instance, in the B♭ Major impromptu on the Rosamunde melody, in Variation No. 2. The relationship of the popular to the romantic in Schubert's art might almost be symbolised by the sequence of Variations 2 and 3 of that impromptu, for No. 3 must be counted one of the finest romantic outbursts in music. Precisely the same can be observed in the E♭ Major Sonata.

2/1 is followed by a highly individual theme, foreshadowing the 'cello melody in the Unfinished Symphony. It is as if Schubert had at once lifted the popularism of 2/1 to a higher plane. There can be no doubt that this exposition is digressive, but it is not a case of premature development.

The development is harmonically very beautiful, but makes scant reference to the material heard before. It is indeed, wholly episodic. This is all the more remarkable because the first group had contained such workable elements. A point of extreme interest is the premature entry, before the recapitulation proper, of 2/2. The recapitulation is practically a repetition of the exposition, though Schubert was aware of the necessity of variation, for 1/1 enters canonically. Moreover, the D♭ draft shows that the development section has been extended in accordance with the demands of proportion, the First Group, too, has been rhythmically braced.

The B Major Sonata (Opus 147) has aroused much comment by its violent wrenching of the tonality. The cavalier nature of 1/1 assists this wrenching nor is the key reached unrelated, being G (the VI♭). This time a rather galumphing treatment of 1/1 provides real development, but the recapitulation brings no variation.

Far more interesting is the first movement of the Sonata in A Minor (Opus 164). Again a magnificently workable first subject is abandoned in favour of an episodic development upon two themes, one a lovely cantabile melody. This movement well repays study. The way in which 2/1, with its floating, hovering character, contrasts with the downward driving music of Group One is beautiful. Important also is its tonality, which is F Major (the VI♭). The recapitulation is conspicuous because 1/1 returns in the subdominant. This, however, is also a feature of Mozart's Sonata in C Major, K. 545. The point becomes important in discussing the Unfinished Symphony.

Space is lacking in which to examine the andantes of these sonatas. The lovely variations of the Andante of Opus 164, probably a homage to a similar movement in the Fourth Symphony of Beethoven, is nevertheless in the vein which is recognised as Schubertian. Its apparent lack of technique suggests rather that it may have possessed orchestral colour in Schubert's imagination.

The peculiar form of the last movements of these sonatas is matter for thought. That of

Opus 164 is neither rondo nor sonata form.
Its principal theme makes its second entry in
the dominant, which distinguishes it from the
rondo, yet it has no development and the
episodic material is repeated after the second
entry. That of the B Major presents similar
problems. The finale of the E♭ Major Sonata
is in sonata form, but its wholly episodic development makes it resemble a rondo to the
ear (the only real test in music). The popular
inspiration of the long episodic fantasia is
interesting. The Biergarten and the Prater
were never more unblushingly brought into
the sonata. There is more in it than this,
however ; the episode, fifty-six bars long,
actually does in miniature what the Wanderer
Fantasia magnificently accomplishes. It presents a half-developed apotheosis of its central
idea, in a restrained bravura passage towards
its close. In the D♭ version this episode only
lasts twenty-five bars, and the bravura passage
occurs in miniscule. It is the singing and
surging impulse which is strongest in Schubert.

A critical summary of Schubert's achievement so far is as follows :

1. His expositions are too full of material,
they do not, strictly speaking, digress or
develop.

2. He has two types of development section. 'Real' development and episodic fantasia. This latter type can be defended by classical reference. The sonatas in G Major and D Major, K. 283 and K. 311, of Mozart and Opus 14 No. 1 of Beethoven are examples.

3. His recapitulations are repetitive of the first section. A brief coda on 1/1 appears in the A Minor Sonata. Both of these features are to be found in the classical masters. The tentative return of a Second Group subject before the First in the E♭ Major Sonata can be paralleled by the K. 311 of Mozart. The First Group tends to recur in the subdominant as in the A Minor and the B Major Sonatas.

4. The tonality relationships are individual and important and associated with romantic impulse.

5. Schubert's proportions do not superficially depart from classical examples more than, say, Mozart departs from his own norm.

These conclusions, however, are for the most part formal and explain little. It will be noticed that the episodic developments are always strongly lyrical in character and similar in feeling to the protracted elements of the exposition. These were already full, not in development, but because lyricism is a char-

acter *which does not easily reduce to a concise utterance.* (Thus the less formal suite has tended
to be the medium of lyrical composers.) It is
quite clear that the introduction of long lyrical
Second Groups was Schubert's difficulty. He
started with subjects of fairly classical type, but
the lyricism of his nature promptly asserted
itself, after which the unlyrical character of his
First Groups prevented him working them. It
was thus the music itself which was straining
the form. For such new wine new bottles
were needed, a too strict adherence to old
forms was indeed Schubert's undoing.

It remains only to say that as romantic
pieces the music is often delightful, and to
point out that it becomes individual during the
period of conflict at Saülengasse.

XIII

THE next period opens in crisis with two abandoned efforts of great interest. A tragedy is contained in the A Minor Sonata of 1823 (Opus 143). Here is an enormous advance in individuality comparable only to the Unfinished Symphony of 1822. The whole of the exposition is full of the most gorgeous opportunities for development. 1/1 breathes a mysteriousness which it has remained for Sibelius to utter. And, as in the Finnish master, the whispered secret suddenly gives rise in 1/2 to an impressive extension which cries aloud for the orchestra. The development opens with the most splendid promise, almost at once achieving grandeur with a *ff* partial statement of the secret, over downward crashing octaves which thrill the player. And then almost at once the music goes to pieces, really, I believe, because the might of the orchestra was needed to support this nobility. Vincent d'Indy has said that this sonata gives the impression of boredom. Despair, rather, is written over the close of its enfeebled development. Opus 143 is a transitional work ; its first movement dismisses the facile lyricism of 1817, the improvisatory andante tells us little, but the twice recurring cantilena episode of the rondo, with its touch of lyrical heroism that foretells Chopin, reminds us of the past.

Of surpassing interest is the little sonata in A Major, of 1825, Opus 120. In this work Schubert solved the problem of the lyrical sonata.

The exposition opens at once with a sweetly flowing melody of rich harmonic texture. All is June fragrance and warmth, too full for spring yet with nothing of the sultriness of summer. The theme sets up its counterstrain at once, containing significant rhythmic elements in both hands. This lovely music continues with the real but placid movement of water until bar 20, when a triplet scale runs up lightly, and entirely without transitional matter the second subject enters. A short transition and 2 enters in the bass below different figuration. The change which has come over 2 is marvellous, there is a gently storming nobility about it which at once sets loose the second transition, rhythmic chords

over a sinking bass, the exposition being con-
cluded by a codetta. There is no heroism
here, but all is pure Schubertian loveliness,
expressed convincingly. The secret is disclosed when we examine the order in which
the themes appear. Instead of introducing
the lyrical quality with the Second Group
Schubert begins straightway with a fully
developed passage of this quality. The impression, aided by the little anacrusis, is that
the music has been going on for some time
before we actually hear it. The stroke was
followed by another equally successful, the
suppression of the transition, which inevitably
would have sounded of scrannel thinness, and
the securing of contrast by different figuration
inside the second subject.

The development does not disappoint. It
begins at once with a sentence of splendid
counterpoint. This sentence of ten bars is
in dimension a miniature, but its musical
content is enormous. The triplet scale is now
converted into upward rushing octave scales,
then references to 2 are combined with figures
of 1 ; a *pp* follows, succeeding which warmth
pours back into the music, and at 80 the
recapitulation begins with 1 in octaves, concluding which a surge in the bass brings fresh

123

interest. It is this little burst which gives the interpretative clue to the rest of the recapitulation, which is just a transposition of the Second Group. The rhythmic chords and the bass may now be allowed to surge more than upon their first appearance ; the effect is splendid. A six-bar coda is full of a restrainedly sentimental poetry, being a recollection of 1, the touch of F♯ Minor in the cadence of the first phrase being perfect.

In the later Schubert there is no real return to this mood. The G Major Sonata of 1826, mistakenly thought to be his best, to some extent reverts to this lyricism in the Second Group. The fine development with its use of both Groups is noteworthy, but the later movements do not make a unity. The reversion to the menuetto shows a retrogressive tendency.

The most vital document for this period is the Unfinished Sonata in C Major of 1825. Since its completion by Ernst Křenek this splendid work should be far better known than it is. There can be no objection to such a service to the composer, some sequential work in the menuetto and the completion of the half-finished rondo alone fell to Dr. Křenek's share. So phenomenal is the history of what I shall call the Principal Theme that no

apology is offered for the following difficult
reading. The second subject will not con-
cern us, nor will harmonic and melodic con-
siderations. By omitting the bar references
I hope to simplify the analysis, but it must
be understood that a detailed examination of
every bar is one of the most valuable disciplines
a Schubertian student can undertake.

Exposition (*of First Subject*)

1. ♩|♩♩♩♩|♩. This is the rhythm of the
first figure of the broad and beautifully symphonic Principal Subject in C Major. Call
the rhythm r^1 and note the starred anacrusis
of one crotchet.

After 20 bars on the Principal Theme transitional work leads back to 1 in a variant form
(1^2) in which the anacrusis is detached, thus :

2. ♪ ᵞ|♩♩♩♩|♩. ♪ ᵞ|♩ etc. (r^2). Sequen-
tial use easily converts r^2 thus.

3. |♩♩♩♩|♩. ♪ ᵞ| (r^3). The star draws
attention to the position of the original
anacrusis. The figure has caught its tail, or
the tail has caught its head. Then the first
bar is dropped and a passage on r^4 follows.

125

4. $\bullet$ $\mathord{\scriptstyle\bullet}$ (r^4).

The second subject is in B Minor. In his first effort Schubert had entered the II♭. The continuity of his work is evident.

Development

The Principal Theme enters in A Major (VI), in a form which we may call 1^3 and with a beautiful melodic appendage, of which the clarinet and flute melody of the first movement of the Unfinished Symphony is the prototype. This r^4 is heard while a most important rhythmic figure in hammered chords enters in the R.H. thus : call it x. Diminished forms, x^2 and r^5, are at once heard, and then x is beaten out by both hands, the R.H. x along growing a tail, the origin of which is at once made apparent by the return of a harmonically reduced Principal Theme in a still further robbed form (r^5). This is a new form of x (x^3). It will be seen that x is really acting as a pulveriser or *solvent* of the Principal Theme. New phrasings and displacements occur which have the effect of disguising the identity of the music. A robbed x^2 appears in the L.H. and with r^6

obtained by simply robbing and displacing r^5, carries on the disintegration of the music. The critical place for the understanding of all this is the third and fourth bars on page seven of the Universal edition. The pulverisation is hereabouts assisted by the tying of the music to the hammered note F$\sharp$. All that is now left of the Principal Theme is a rhythmic insistence on F$\sharp$ in both hands. Finally, the R.H. x begins to weaken, it loses dynamic force and becomes robbed until at last all that is left of the great Principal Theme and its solvent is ♫ ♪ . The little tail never disappears. Suddenly the F$\sharp$s swell in volume, are taken as the dominant of B Major, and the Principal Theme in form 1^3 rides in with glorious effect.

But this enormously simplified demonstration of a severely intellectual process does not exhaust the interest of this movement. This return may be said to mark the commencement of the recapitulation, inasmuch as the second subject appears in A Minor. But now the transitional matter sinks to a mysterious hush which has *always* the same purpose in Schubert. The bass boldly descends a third, and the Principal Theme enters in A♭ Major

(VI ♭). This may be called the coda, but it contains further telescoped reference to the transitional matter, after which a final *pp* and a beautifully retarded reference to the theme closes the movement.

Now the classical terms fit this process inconveniently. So described, the recapitulation starts with the theme in the flat tonic (!) ; moreover, it never really achieves the tonic until the final bars, nor do all its elements appear until the A ♭ Major section is opened. Throughout the movement the second subject has played a purely formal part, and every device demonstrates that we are being told the history of one theme. Omitting reference to the second subject we have this schema :

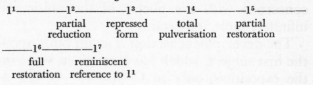

1^1————1^2————1^3————1^4————1^5————

partial   repressed   total   partial
reduction   form   pulverisation   restoration

————1^6————1^7

full   reminiscent
restoration   reference to 1^1

In so far as it is a one-theme history, the Wanderer Fantasia, that earliest and best of symphonic poems, is at once called to mind.

It has been held that Schubert was incapable of the intellectual effort of the severe forms. In the light of this sonata the contention is reduced to an illiteracy.

No space can be spared for the fine sonata in D of 1825 (Opus 53), but perhaps as the history of the Principal Subject of the first movement is in some ways similar to that of the C Major, the unworthiness of its second subject may be explained. Schubert was little interested in second subjects at this period. They are almost formal relics.

The C Major Sonata once understood, the Opus 42 in A Minor becomes the key to the later Schubert. Vincent d'Indy, who dismisses Schubert and Brahms as symphonists with three and four lines apiece, admits of this sonata that it will withstand formal criticism. The general agreement of French critics shows that d'Indy was infallible, so that we can be concerned with the poetry of the music, of infinitely more importance.

The development section is again built upon the first subject, which has been given twice in the exposition, once in C Minor. At first a reduced form is used, and then a second reduction of exquisite tenderness enters over a gently rocking accompaniment, itself a softened version of the rhythmic clash of the transition. What follows is some of the most magical poetry in all music.

Beneath R.H. tremolo chords a reduced

version of the theme has been sounding with
a strange suggestion of horn timbre ; far below
a significant bass mutters. The horns grow
more insistent and a resonant A is heard in
the bass. Then the horns, hastening first to
enunciate their fragment of the theme, answer
the bass by calling A twice, with astonishing
and disturbing effect. Again the horns answer
the summons of the bass, even more bewilder-
ing this time than before. A♯ sounds below,
and without waiting to interpose the theme,
the horns press forward with two A♯s. Immediately B calls out of the depths, the bass has
begun to climb, the effect is one of the utmost
excitement as the horns make B heard twice.
C in the bass peals loudly. All this has been
splendid, but now a stroke of superlative genius
is made. To the resounding C out of the
depths the horns reply hesitantly or as if waiting, after which there is no voice below, the
bass is absent. Straightway the tremolo chords
weaken, and as they do so the bass calls C♯ ;
quietly the horns reply C♯. The musical sus-
pense is almost unbearable as once again the
bass is missing. The R.H. figures become
weaker still, and just as they are fading away
C♯ is whispered twice, not from the bass but
from the mid octave. It is as if the horns had

crept down to the brink of the abyss and were calling to someone far below.

There is no answer. A moment's silence and then the poignant beauty of the theme breathes softly in F♯ Minor.

Nothing so much betrays Berlioz as his unimaginative condemnation of the famous early entry of the horn in the first movement of the Eroica ; similarly nothing so much exposes Liszt as his suggestion that the horn calls in this passage should be amplified with chords.

Three things must be noticed :

(*a*) All this magic is *severely practical*. It may be regarded as a carefully planned return to the tonic.

(*b*) The technique is in essence that of the C Major Sonata.

(*c*) Development is not complex elaboration but *evocation*. This is fundamental.

This period also sees the deepening in significance of the andantes, in itself an advance towards the spiritual unity of the whole sonata, a problem not yet solved. The long and lovely andante of the D Major sets a new type.

Summarising this examination of the period 1818-1825 we may say :

1. The romantic-lyrical impulse has achieved

its convincing expression, and in great measure disappears.

2. There is some redundancy in exposition and recapitulation, and this is due to adherence to old forms. The diminished rôle of the second subject demanded a compression of transitional material.

3. There is no weakness in development, if complexity be not sought. A pure musicality of evocatory type is Schubert's aim.

4. There is a continuous growth from 1815 to 1825. The very idiom of the Opus 42 beauty can be found in the F♯ Minor fragment of 1817.

5. The spiritual unity of the sonata is being realised.

XIV

THE first two periods are logical divisions, the third is not so, but is closed by arbitrary Death.

After 1826 Schubert produced no pianoforte works in sonata form until the creative frenzy of 1828 informed him. This takes us beyond the point we have reached in his life ; nevertheless we must examine the three sonatas of September 1828.

The C Minor Sonata must be passed over with brief mention. It is really of indeterminate type, and marks a tentative return to Sturm und Drang. Its development is episodic and its last movement inordinately long. Schubert must have been drunk with musical excitement in this astonishing month, and it must have seemed to him that the only thing to do with a life that had so failed of normal achievement was to surrender it entirely to music. There are fine things in the Sonata in C Minor, but there are better things ahead.

The last, the popular B♭ Sonata, contains

one of the most masterly returns to the first subject in the history of the form. The development which is in part episodic, begins with the lovely 1/1 in C♯ Minor. It is important to notice that the melody begins from the mediant of the scale, and not from the tonic as in the exposition. Very soon it disappears, and while the L.H. is filling up with useful harmonies the R.H. begins to sing snatches of melody. But out of the L.H. a new and supremely beautiful theme develops and shortly dominates the music. If I were asked to put my finger upon some passage exclusively Schubertian, it would be this and not one of the lovely cantabiles. The music progresses like a boat over regular waves, a dip into deep chords on the strong beat and a little flurry of sprayed quavers in the rest of the bar. Then comes a burst of excitement which carries the music into D Minor, which, be it noted, is the mediant tonality to B♭ Major. Now the episodic theme returns above a line of reiterated chords in D Minor, then below it, whereupon the outburst is repeated in a reduced form. At once the thunder roll of 1/1 is heard in the bass, resolving on D, whereupon the Principal Theme floats in in D Minor, at the mediant position. The thunder rumbles again and B♭ emerges, when the melody enters again in the tonic key. Had Schubert begun his recapitulation here it still would have been very beautiful, but a greater loveliness ensues. The thunder peals softly and now settles on D, in the minor mode of which the melody re-enters. A few trailing phrases, and the music dies away. A silence, and the theme enters with all its original breadth of harmony in B♭ Major.

The justness of the episodic development can now be seen. The effect of that return would never have been so wonderful had we heard it in all the tonalities of development. The rhythmic structure and the hastening character of the episode show that its whole purpose is to excite expectation. Once again the development is poetic and dramatic rather than elaborative. The part that tonality plays in the art of Schubert becomes apparent. Here it is doing the whole work of the development, with perfect success. The sudden entry into C♯ Minor from F Major at the outset is of exquisite poignancy. The marvellous melodic phrase is inestimably heightened in beauty by just that choice of key, as criminal experiment in dark secrecy will prove. There is nothing in music more simply lovely than the interplay of D Minor and B♭ Major at the close, and textual elaboration would utterly destroy it.

The profound Andante with its striving towards the major mode is a further advance which unfortunately the last two movements do not sustain, despite their beauty.

Greater spiritual unity is achieved by the A Major Sonata of this year. A lovely but repetitive opening movement is followed by a romantic and wholly Schubertian Andante of delicate charm in which the varied sentence lengths are the most interesting technical feature. A short but vivid and highly prophetic scherzo precedes the rondo which concludes the sonata. For the first time in Schubert the last movement appears as the emotional climax. It is remarkable that it is a rondo which achieves this, until we remember that Schubert has reached supreme heights with the return of a theme, the essential characteristic of a rondo.

The quiet serenity of the Principal Melody unmistakably set the spiritual key. After a first episode both long and beautiful, the first return of the melody is managed with consummate skill. It is the melody itself which is now developed, and splendidly. A nobly raging but restrained bravura passage leads to a remarkable apotheosis of the melody in the minor mode. The sombre majesty of this passage is immense, but the sheer poetry of the next return far surpasses it in beauty. A new transition is begun at once (bar 180) ; above and below broken chords fragments of melody converse. The important matter is that the harmony persistently follows the melody. Then, just as the bass authoritatively fixes the tonality by delivering a phrase built on the subdominant, dominant and tonic of C♯ Major, the upper melody moves on to D natural. For the first time the harmony does not follow, but rises no further than F♯ Minor. The bass becomes sterner and announces the tonic mediant and dominant of this tonality, and once again the upper melody strains away. The harmony refuses to advance and the bitter-sweet dissonance is heard again. Immediately the bass outlines the chord of F♯ Minor with increased authority, and this time the upper melody submissively repeats F♯, A and C♯, after which, marvellous stroke, it is heard no more. Then the harmony itself sinks slowly into silence with that same dissonance of C♯ and D muffled in the bass. The effect is overwhelming when that C♯ is taken as the dominant of F♯ Major and the Principal Melody floats with indescribable serenity in the remote tonality, from which it slowly moves to the tonic.

It is here that we can take leave of description safely. It will be seen that Schubert is exploring the very depths of musical psychology. His greatest beauties will always be found to rest upon some subtle psychological truth, which is not to say a programme. If this be challenged, the B♭ Major Sonata provides a ready instance. The whole of the episodic development rests upon a spiritual verity which can be symbolised thus :

A hastening journey towards the land, the burst of excitement when the far-off island is sighted and the redoubled speed. The second exultation, but quelled at once, as through the shore mists all that longed-for peace is seen, and the hesitation and hovering uncertainty of the premature return. It is a dramatic schema which underlies universal experience.

Transfer the schema of this return of the A Major Rondo to any field of human experience, and it is valid. Society may accept as justified all forms of evil, poverty, injustice and war, as it does. It may evolve beautiful religions to salve the unappeasable pain ; it may strive to shackle the onward speeding

138

spirit of man, it may crush out rebellion and idealism as it did and does in Schubert's Vienna, but only at the expense of a hidden dissonance which invades the very bass of society and which Art alone can for a while transfigure. Or in the individual spirit the schema of this rondo seems to tell of one who, by misused liberty, brought into his own being a sharp and inexorable dissonance, as of incurable disease, and out of that dissonance fashioned a music of serenity. It is only a counterfeit biography which needs to be labelled ' A Hero's Life.'

No just summary of this period can be made. Formally it sees a rebirth of the Second Group with attendant problems. It is clear that Schubert has not yet found his own forms, though his aesthetic and method are clear. What he really needed was public understanding, generous criticism from revering scholars, and some security against the wolf which drove him to compose ceaselessly for a few pence. The genius which can create a symphony or three sonatas in a month would surely have evolved the forms necessary for his music. The greatest of his life's ironies is that the tide of critical opinion was actually about to turn.

Aestheticians may value a final remark.
The mingling of the classic and the romantic
in Schubert's art can be perfectly evaluated
in this : he approaches the true romantic
task of spiritual analysis precisely in that
matter of the return of a theme, a problem
dictated by classical form. This might well
be made the starting point of a fresh assault
upon the baffling problem of the nature of Art.

XV

THE view of Schubert's development so far obtained is largely confirmed by a study of the chamber music and symphonies.

The first period of quartet writing, dated from 1812, yielded eleven quartets, composed principally for the home quartet. They have been too promptly dismissed as derivative works ; they contain indeed a deal of good music and interesting experimentation in form. In the latter respect the D Major Quartet of 1813 is worthy of analysis.

An important feature is early noticeable. Schubert does not treat his four instruments as abstract and individual voices, like the later Beethoven. The grouping of them into pairs is a special feature which lends romantic and at times orchestral colour to his chamber music.

The symphonies of this period reinforce these remarks. Characteristics of his later scoring are visible from the beginning. It is the clarinet which gives out the first subject of the Third Symphony. The Fifth, of Sep-

tember 1816, is by far the best of these early
works. Understanding of the Unfinished Symphony is assisted by two observations ; all
these early symphonies, with the exception of
the Fifth, begin with the traditional adagio.
The first subject of the Tragic Symphony,
No. 4, is never recapitulated in the tonic key.

Two transitional quartets mark the year
1817 (E Major and E♭ Major, Opus 125),
after which Schubert abandoned the medium
until 1820, when he wrote the fine and purely
individual movement in C Minor. This was
not the first work to achieve real liberation of
personality. The justly popular Trout Quintet,
which sets out to be no more than lovely music
and succeeds perfectly, had been written at
Steyr in Upper Austria while Schubert was
on tour with Vogl. Art upon occasion pro-
duces its curious appositions. The Trout
Quintet, written at the request of a comfortable bourgeois, owes its origin to a poem of
the revolutionary Schubart, who spent ten
years of misery in a fortress prison. The four-
handed Variations which Schubert dedicated
to the republican Beethoven are upon a melody
composed by Josephine's daughter, La Reine
Hortense, pawn of the traitor Napoleon.

It will be remembered that a good deal of

partly realised work precedes the apex of this period. 1822, the date of the Unfinished Symphony, indicates its relationship to the works that might have been created when Schubert's powers were at their height in 1825, had the world of music gone out to meet him. This symphony, the manuscript of which was sent to a musical society at Gratz as reward for Schubert's election as an honorary member, lay at Hüttenbrenner's house, undiscovered until 1865. Whether the symphony was ever intended to contain more than two movements has been warmly debated. The Allegro and the Andante certainly make a unity, and this could not be said of any other two movements of Schubert. A few bars of a projected Scherzo exist, and this, I think, must be taken as conclusive. The following view deserves attention, for it reconciles the unfinished state of the work with Hüttenbrenner's curious possession of the manuscript. The first two movements were sent as a feeler ; Schubert, always eager for performance when the chance was presented, could not stay to complete the work. It is wholly consistent with his character that he should have suspended composition of the Scherzo and Allegro Vivace until news was received that the Gratz society had placed the work in rehearsal. The composition and scoring of these movements would only have been a matter of a few days to such a mind as Schubert's, aflame with the joy of recognition. But the society did not respond, and Hüttenbrenner, both for shame and to avoid humiliating his friend (and perhaps covetous of the treasure in his hands) did not return the manuscript. If this be so, then that the B Minor Symphony is unfinished is the fault of the piffling cudgel-biters of Gratz.

But they must be forgiven : the Vienna Society even refused to admit Schubert as a viola player on the grounds that he was a professional.

Even to-day the Unfinished is occasionally misunderstood. It has actually been suggested that the opening theme is an afterthought to the clarinet and flute melody, which thus becomes the Principal Theme. The plain and audible fact is that the opening bars give out the very germ of the whole movement. It is a refined expression of the idea behind the early opening adagios. The case that this theme does not return in the tonic until the coda shows that the symphony is in line with an oft-repeated procedure, as readers of this book will understand. The beauty of the development is absolutely characteristic, as is the method.

At the close of the exposition, and instead of coming to rest upon the expected note, the theme goes on down another four notes with marvellous disclosure of unexpected depths; the feeling of mystery is intense. Immediately a figure of the same theme is heard pleadingly in the first violins, while drear bassoon tones support the cold violas in a self-counterpoint. Then follows a crescendo which is for all men's hearing a concentration of this appeal. The pleading rises to a climax ff on the sombre majesty of the C ♯ Minor chord. Now to those who have paid heed to the doctrine of tonality this will be a significant key. The second subject, the glorious 'cello melody, had entered in G Major, which from B is the VI. From E Minor we have now reached C ♯ Minor, the VI also. Straightway the accompaniment to the second subject is heard, but, poetic stroke, the 'cellos withhold their melody, and as if to show that they are not absent they join with the other strings in touching the strong beats.

The acute listener perceives more than this. The eerie tonality and the suggestive timbres make this a pleading, so that further reference to 1/1 is not necessary as a prelude to a fresh crisis of appeal. Again the accompaniment to 2 is heard, the 'cellos withholding their theme. The appeal is made a third time, and then the full orchestra replies with a *ff* statement of the Principal Theme in the subdominant. But of which theme are these allusions to 2 developments? Surely in the name of all that is musical they are revelations about 1! Elsewhere in the Opus 42 we have heard fragments of a theme make an intense appeal which was answered by a restatement of the theme itself. That the theme returns in the subdominant does not disprove that it is the principal member; the A Minor and B Major Sonatas of 1817, the Tragic Symphony and numerous other instances of this can be given to show that Schubert regarded a subdominant appearance as formally equivalent of a tonic. The absence of textual elaboration must not be allowed to confuse; the added poignancy which 1 has now gained is itself development, of a poetic kind. Another fifty bars working brings 1/2 with which the recapitulation may be said to begin, it being almost the sole object of this section, at this period of Schubert's life, to restate the Second Group in the tonic. A coda upon the Principal Theme brings the movement to a close.

Upon this understanding the proportions of the Allegro become exceedingly symmetrical.

Exposition	Development	Recapitulation	Coda
110 bars	108 bars	110 bars	41 bars

Moreover, a comparison of the history of the Principal Theme with that of the Unfinished Sonata in C Major and the D Major of 1825 shows that the Unfinished is part of a definite tendency in Schubert's art.

Of a mass of fine achievement in this period lack of space prohibits mention. The lovely A Minor Quartet of late 1823 or early 1824 shows formal advance. The centre of gravity has now moved to the menuetto, introduced by the preludial phrase of *Die Götter Griechenlands*, a regret for vanished gods. As in the song, the effect is greatly assisted by the interplay of major and minor modes, an idiom which helps the plain man, who recognises the pathos of the alternation, to love the work of Schubert. Lest cynics scoff, it should be added that scientifically the plain man is wholly right. The word pathos, of course, is used in the sense of its Greek root. The Andante upon the gracious melody which appears in the

Rosamunde music, written for von Chezy's failure in 1823, is conspicuous for its delightful counterpoint and permits us to ask what Schubert's contrapuntal achievements might have been after his course of lessons, begun a few days before his death.

A little-known work of these years, the sonata for arpeggione and pianoforte, has been finely scored as a 'cello concerto by the Spanish 'cellist, Gaspar Cassadó.   Its sheer beauty, rollicking good spirits and the scarcity of 'cello concertos entitles one to plead for its perform-ance in this form.

The finest of the Schubert quartets, the D Minor (Death and the Maiden), is usually attributed to 1826, but had been first sketched in 1824.   All the maturity of 1825 is thus summed up in it.   It is the spiritual unity of the quartet which impresses most, and it is noteworthy that the centre of tension is now the variations movement, and as in the C Major Symphony, the extraordinary Scherzo is fol-lowed by a ceaselessly driving finale.   In pro-fundity of feeling, but without any appearance of a programme such as fanciful critics have discovered in the D Minor, the great G Major Quartet of 1826, with its daring tonality scheme, stands side by side with the Death

and the Maiden Quartet.   Orchestral feeling
is pushed to its limits in this work.

The D Minor Quartet in some ways foretells the C Major Quintet of that amazing
September of 1828.   It is the finest of Schubert's works for strings.   The enigmatic tonalities and the pathos of the Adagio, a rare
movement in Schubert, and the unprecedented
grief of the Trio, speak of rapidly growing
profundity.

Nothing in this earlier music permits us to
expect such a splendour as that of the C Major
Symphony of March 1828.   Its white magnifi-
cence is not only new to Schubert, but to all
music.   It is at once the secular and the vastly
more mystical counterpart of Palaestrina's
cloistral loveliness, unintelligible without a cult.
And as if to emphasise the point, the symphony
largely achieves its effects by sheer intoxica-
tion of persistent rhythms, an element only
smuggled into the Italian's art.   The fineness
of the music, however, has obscured for many
the aesthetic basis of the work, a basis which
demanded length and justified repetitiveness.

The whole of the Allegro is one vast exercise
in rhythmic exploitation.   The first subject
has often been criticised, unjustly.   It serves
perfectly as a liberator of a steely, racing

rhythm, the mere exterior shape returning only with perfunctory formality. Again, the sudden and unheralded entry of the beautiful second subject, with its own special rhythmic contribution, discloses the aesthetic basis. In this Allegro there must be no slackening of pace in pulseless transitions. The Scherzo even more unambiguously proclaims its object, and with a modernity still surprising in its suggestion of some magnificent piece of glittering machinery. The image, deliberately chosen, may dismay a few aesthetic weaklings. Again the second subject is introduced breathlessly, and at once its externals are stripped off, so that already in bar 41 the naked, scintillating ardour of string timbre is swinging up and down with enormous power. Even this rhythmic form is later simplified so that the music rises and falls with immense suggestion of a shining piston crosshead and rod, driving an exultant music through time and space.

The same is true of the Allegro Vivace. In a certain sense this is not Art, for there is no music which gives such a revelation of astronomic grandeur in its eternal, pulsing sameness of beauty. It is precisely its alleged defect which is its strength. Just as the time scale of the whole symphony is perfectly indicated

by the immediate wood-wind repetition of
the opening horn theme, so that discerning
miniaturists ought at once to walk out, the
leaping into life of that triplet figure and its
15-bar outlining of the chord C Major, tells
us that an ordinary product of the musical
textile industry is not to be expected. It is
the termination of this music which is so awe-
inspiring. When once the recapitulation of
the second subject is behind, the huge *fff*
climax sinks rapidly to a *ppp* ; it is the old
idiom of the return. There is no slackening
of pace as the triplet figure begins to create
one of the most astonishing splendours in
music. It is as if we were borne up on that
pulsating atom of rhythm, above the world
and out from its limits over the cold purity
of universal space, as if we beheld the circling
of worlds and the laws they manifest. Again
and again we are lifted with such excitement
that we do not notice it is the means of chang-
ing tonality which is being used ; the pealing
joy of the wood-wind after every upsoaring
flight only serves to exhilarate us more.

I suppose no man hearing this music can
escape that sense of witnessing the universe
of unseen law and shining constellation. The
object of all this length is disclosed, the uni-

verse itself is repetitive ; no precise and ordered work of art could have worked this miracle of vision, in comparison with which Palaestrina only illustrates a dogma. The mighty impetus disclosed in the first Allegro has worked itself out in an experience not to be found elsewhere in music.

Neglected, misesteemed, unrewarded, Franz Schubert died in the year of this achievement.

XVI

THE most important European event of 1827 was the death of Beethoven, at whose funeral Schubert was a torch-bearer. With Anselm Hüttenbrenner he had already visited the dying master, who towards the end had taken pleasure in Schubert's songs. 'Truly there is in this Schubert a divine spark,' Beethoven may be believed to have said, though all things are confused by the erratic Schindler, his factotum. There is no doubt that Beethoven's death affected Schubert deeply ; early admiration had deepened to an awed reverence in these later years. Upon the return from the graveside at Währing, Franz and his friends stopped at a tavern. Lifting his glass, he gave the toast of the departed composer and then called for homage to ' the one who will be the next.'

Friends were now beginning to drift away. Schwind had gone to Munich, Spaun and Kupelwieser had married, while even the elderly Vogl had taken a pupil for bride.

Nevertheless, the Schubertiaden continued to be held. In general it was a time of poverty, and we hear of Schubert subsisting on rolls at Bognor's café and of gentle requests to his stepmother to look into the long stocking. The Frölich sisters were much in contact with Franz at this period, and it was at Anna's request that he composed a birthday serenade for one of her friends, she having nothing else to give. At its performance he was absent, having forgotten the work, an offence he repeated a while later when the *Serenade* was to be given publicly. This time Anna burst into tears, and a friend, after tactful pretence at hard thinking, suggested that he was perhaps to be found at the Oak Tree, whose good beer made it popular with musicians, he added. The friend shortly returned with the delinquent Franz.

In September, upon his return from Gratz, whither he had been invited by the Pachlers, a well-to-do family of musical amateurs, he immediately fell ill. His symptoms—vertigo, pain in the arm, violent headaches and moments of partial blindness—reveal that it was an outbreak of the old enemy. It was during the resultant depression that he worked furiously upon the *Winterreise* songs. Upon their conclusion he sang them to a group of his friends, who were unanimously dismayed by their gloom.

A fee of 100 florins for some eucharistic anthems relieved Schubert's distress, but he was at one time driven to listen to the windy bore, Rocklitz, who desired him to set to music a poem of his, already rejected by Beethoven and Weber. Rocklitz, a musical critic, like the young persons at the Russian ballet, knew all about it and about. He instructed Schubert that the music was to open *ff*, after which was to follow a long *sostenuto* for horns, clarinets, etc. Schubert agreed that it would sound very well, but omitted to write the music.

When 1828 opened Franz was living with Schober in his rooms at the Blue Hedgehog. About this time, and like Beethoven, he came under the influence of Handel, several volumes having been presented to him. It is difficult to imagine one of the serenest symphonic musics of all time being composed in a room above the worldly noise of a tavern, but in March the C Major Symphony was written.

It is here that a comparison between Schubert and his idol Beethoven may be attempted. It is by the greatest of forms in the most formidable of mediums that a man is tested, and in music this means the quartet and the symphony. At thirty-one years of age Beethoven had only composed his first symphony in C, while Schubert had already completed nine. Dismissing seven of them, this leaves the Unfinished and the C Major as his first and second attempts. Will it be denied that these two works show as great an individuality as the first and second of Beethoven? More than this is certain. The vision of the C Major Finale is in aesthetic type higher than even the Eroica or the Fifth in C Minor. And if the perfection of form of these two works places them higher in musicianly esteem, as is just, could it be expected that such a mighty influx of splendour could be reduced to an order devised for music of quite another species? Certainly not by one so despised by the musical world that not even this work could secure performance. It is hard to believe that the orchestra of the Society of Music Friends to whom it was offered found the work too difficult. The loss of an audition to a mind struggling with this whelming inspiration cannot be estimated by those of us who pause over the placing of a comma.

It was Bauernfeld who persuaded Franz to give his only public concert of his works. It was a difficult task to convince him of the possibility of profit or esteem, yet the concert, given upon the first anniversary of Beethoven's death, produced £32 for the composer. It is perfectly clear that public taste was ahead of official criticism, for the salon of the Hedgehog next door to the Blue, red in colour, was packed. With an earnest request to repeat the event Schubert characteristically failed to comply.

He made unsatisfactory efforts to sell works to the firm of Schotts in February. It is a little staggering to think that one could have secured the manuscript and copyright of the Death and the Maiden Quartet for about one hundred florins at this time. Probst, also approached by Schubert, capably demonstrated the truth of the law of supply and demand by beating him down to 17s. 6d. for the E♭ Trio, Opus 100. Rather than inflict his poverty upon Schober any longer he left the Blue Hedgehog, and in October his correspondence with Schott was addressed from The Town of Ronsperg. The Mainz publisher, however, refused to pay more than thirty florins for a fine four-part choral work, and returned the famous Impromptus as too difficult and unlikely to sell in France.

Many times he had sworn to compose no more unprofitable songs, but at the mercy of inexorable genius he wrote the first thirteen of the *Schwanengesang* in August, a mass and numerous other works engaging his leisure. With care, comfort and reasonable health such exhaustion of impetus as this must imply might have no serious consequences. But as things were, some serious prostration was almost certain to ensue.

In October Schubert began to sicken, and upon the advice of his physician went to live in the rural suburb of Neue Wiedern, at the house of brother Ferdinand, with whom he shortly went upon a three-days' walking tour. Amongst other things they visited the grave of Haydn. Upon his return Franz complained of excessive fatigue, but nothing in his behaviour awakened alarm until one night, while supping at a tavern and having begun a plate of fish, he flung down his knife and fork with the cry that he had been poisoned. The following day, however, he walked to Hernals to hear one of his brother's compositions, a requiem mass.

Prophetic forebodings of death are the

quaint delight of the novelist, yet despite sundry gloomy remarks Schubert was clearly facing the future with thought of music. It is intensely interesting that he actually began to study counterpoint with Sechter in these days ; such an equipment would have been of immense value to him. But, ominously, since the night of his alarm concerning poison he was eating nothing and complaining of fatigue. Soon his temperature began to rise.

On the 12th of November he wrote a startling letter to Schober : ' I am ill. I have had nothing to eat or drink for eleven days and can only stagger uncertainly between chair and bed. If I take any food at all I cannot keep it down. Come to my rescue in this desperate condition with something to read.'

Beethoven's last craving had been for wine and yet more wine of renowned vintages. Schubert asks for more of Fennimore Cooper, whose ' Last of the Mohicans ' he had just read.

He spoke affectionately of his little step-sister Josefa, who nursed him at this stage of his illness, and when Spaun visited him a few days later he was correcting the proofs of the second half of the *Winterreisse* and still planning

the music to the *Count of Gleichen*. Then, pos-
sibly because his physician fell ill, new doctors
were engaged. Nevertheless, as one of these
doctors was a specialist in venereal disease, it
is probable that a treatment was prescribed
appropriate to the nervous fever of the advanced disease. Bauernfeld, who visited Franz
on the afternoon of the 17th, has recorded
that he found him weak, fevered and fearfully
depressed, but without delirium.

The same evening a raving delirium took
possession of him and, too late, it became
evident that he was in the grip of a virulent
typhus.

The following day Ferdinand and the male
nurse were continually engaged in struggling
to keep the terrified Franz in bed. ' Tell me
what is happening,' he whispered in horror at
one moment. ' What are they doing with
me ? ' Ferdinand could only comfort him
with stumbling words. Several hours passed
while the exhausted body lay inertly burning
away.

Suddenly Franz began to struggle madly
upon the bed and shrieked, ' Put me in my
own room, don't leave me in this corner under
the ground ! Do I not deserve a place on
earth ? ' They fought desperately to restrain

him, striving to assure him that he was not being buried alive. 'You *are* in your own room and lying on your bed,' pleaded Ferdinand.

'No, it is not true,' was the answer; '*Beethoven is not lying here.*'

What ghastly confusion made havoc of his mind we can only shrinkingly surmise. But the revelation of affinity in that last utterance must not be ignored. 'No, it is not true'—he declares that he is being buried, which is normally a sign of death. He fears that he is dead, and his mind leaps onward to a greater terror—of loneliness, for there should have been one, a mightier brother than Ferdinand, awaiting him with a smile, a bottle of good vintage and a sheaf of music-paper, the Beethoven towards whom he had driven his life in that last ecstasy of creation.

Or interpreting otherwise, both phrases of his cry may become a denial that he is alive, and the proof of death is that Beethoven, long dead, is not there. The principle of life is Beethoven. Upon any interpretation approximation to the greatest master of all is evident.

The 19th of November witnessed the continuance of the drama ; the delirium was weaker but less interrupted by lucidity, and

L 161

even when he spoke his disorganised speech lacked meaning. In one of these intervals of stupor or exhaustion the sacrament was administered. Soon after midday he quietly put out his hand and clutched at the wall, murmured with perfect clarity, ' Here is my end,' and sank into a deep prostration which resembled sleep.

Towards three o'clock on the 19th of November 1828 Franz Schubert died.

Life and Death are not disposed to play out their matters with the restraint of artistry. There was no need for final irony. They dressed Franz in the habit of a friar, and placed a crucifix in his hands, and buried him at Während, not far from Beethoven.

And after the burial there was that business to perform with which men instinctively steady themselves after loss, the disposal of his property. The sum of his worth was fifty shillings, and a bundle of manuscripts, amongst which must have been many of the great works of the last year, was valued at 8s. 6d.

This does not sound like Reality. It was not. The whole lesson of this man's life is that mankind has not yet achieved that ideal.

GLOSSARY

Anacrusis.

That part of a phrase which precedes the first strong beat, to which it thus gives emphasis. If, when you are angered, you say tut | tút tut | tút, the first tut is an anacrusis. Or listen to a wood-pigeon's call.

Rondo.

The essence of the rondo is indicated by the following schema. There are many more complicated forms.

A. A melody in tonic key.

B. A second melody called an episode in some other key, *e.g.* the dominant (V).

A. The melody again, in tonic key.

B. The episode again, in tonic key.

A. The melody in tonic key.

Or, in other words, *A* is the tune which goes round and round and sometimes under and over, and *B* is the mulberry bush, but it is not always the same bush. It may become a tree or a whole shrubbery, or a gardener who walks away.

Scale.

The notes of a scale have these names : Tonic, Supertonic, Mediant, Subdominant, Dominant, Submediant, Leading note, Tonic. The tonic key is the tonality the composer declares his piece to be ' in.' If you are playing in C and the music enters the key of G, you have moved to the dominant (V), if to F then to the subdominant (IV). If you are forced into B, it may be the flat tonic or the seventh, but it is equally annoying either way.

Scherzo.

Literally a ' joke,' but not an ' absurdity,' as some moderns have thought. Occasionally it borders on horseplay, and it contains a contrasting interlude called a Trio.

Sonata Form.

Its essence is indicated by this schema :

Exposition, in which the themes are given out. It contains two groups, thus :

1. One or more remarks in tonic key, leading to
2. One or more statements in some other key.

Development, in which all or some of the thoughts of 1 or 2 or both are argued in a new light. Or they may be omitted and fresh remarks made. The latter procedure is thought by some to be rude.

Recapitulation, in which the material of the first section is restated. The Second Group is brought to the tonic key. Sometimes argument breaks out afresh, or parts of the exposition are left out as understood. Often there is a parting shot called a coda. This can be very effective with persons of genius.

BIBLIOGRAPHY

MODERN and essential works only are given.

THE SOURCES

1. DEUTSCH, O. E. *Franz Schubert : Die Doku-mente seines Lebens und Schaffens*. 2 vols. 1913.

2. *Franz Schubert. Letters and other Writings*. Edited by O. E. DEUTSCH. Translated by V. SAVILE. 1928.

BIOGRAPHIES

3. DAHMS, WALTER. *Schubert*. 1912. The best German Life.

4. FLOWER, NEWMAN. *Franz Schubert*. 1928. Easily the best full-length study in English. Contains a copious bibliography.

5. KOBALD, KARL. *Franz Schubert and his Times*. 1928. Translated by B. MARSHALL.

6. Article in Grove.

ON THE MUSIC

7. CAPELL, RICHARD. *The Songs of Schubert*. 1928. A scholarly and enthusiastic work. By far the best book on the subject in any language.

8. KOELTSZCH, H. *Franz Schubert in seinen Klavier Sonaten.* 1927.

9. SMITH, ALEXANDER. *Schubert (The Symphonies).* 1926. The Musical Pilgrim Series. Brief analyses of the Unfinished and C Major Symphonies.

10. 'Schubert.' Article in W. W. Cobbett's *Cyclopedic Survey of Chamber Music.* 2 vols. 1929-30.

11. TOVEY, DR. DONALD. 'Schubert.' An Essay in the *Heritage of Music.* Edited by HUBERT J. FOSS. 1927.

12. TOVEY, DR. DONALD. Article on Tonality in Schubert's music. *Music and Letters.* October 1928.

The last two essays are fundamental. The foundations of Schubertian scholarship in this country. Or see articles by Dr. Tovey on Harmony, Sonata Form, Rondo, etc., in the *Encyclopædia Britannica*.

I have used the Breitkopf and Härtel edition of the music.

INDEX

Alexander I, of Russia, 55

Barbaja, 75
Bauernfeld, 54, 84, 86, 92, 157, 159
Beethoven, 9, 11, 13, 20, 21, 22, 23, 39, 55, 57, 65, 67, 68, 81, 87, 90, 94, 95, 113, 119, 155, 156, 157, 159
Benedict, Julius, afterwards Sir, 69
Bergreen, and Ludlam's Cave, 68

Castelli, I., 68, 69, 70
Chezy, Countess von, 77
Chezy, Wilhelm von, 76, 77, 148
Congress of Vienna, 34
Convict, School, 24, 25, 29, 33, 42

Diabelli, 67, 83

Esterhazy, Count, 59, 60, 61
Esterhazy, Caroline, 60, 81, 82

Franz II, 9, 10, 12, 20, 51, 56, 90

Frölich Sisters, 66, 76, 91, 154
Frölich, Anna, 154
Frölich, Kathi, 66, 76, 91

Gmunden, 87, 91
Goethe, 12, 95
Graz Musical Society, 143, 144
Grillparzer, 66, 68
Grob, Theresa, 42, 43, 45
Grob, Widow, 42

Handel, 155, 158
Hauschka, 68
Haydn, 27, 39
Holzapfel, 27
Holzer, M., 18, 23, 38, 42
Hüttenbrenner, Anselm, 89, 153
Hüttenbrenner, Josef, 59, 66, 86, 143, 144

Jewish Synagogue, 41
Joseph II, 9, 20

Kärntnerthor theatre, 75
Korner, 24
Křenek, 124
Kupelwieser, 75, 153

Lang, Dr., 21, 25, 42
Leopold II, 10
Lichtenthal church, 18
Ludlam's Cave, 68, 69

Maria Theresa (wife of Franz
  II), 13
Mass in F, 38, 39, 43
  in B♭, 39
  in G, 39
  in A♭, 40
  in E♭, 40
Mayrhofer, J., 49, 52, 54, 63,
  86, 92, 96, 97, 98, 99, 100,
  105
Metternich, 9, 55
Milder, Anna, 89
Moonshine House, 86, 87
Moscheles, 68, 69
Mozart, 9, 21, 27, 39, 48, 57,
  114, 119

Naderers, 11
Nägeli, publisher, 91

Probst, publisher, 91

Rio, del, family of, 87
Rocklitz, 155
Rondo. See Glossary
Rosamunde, 77, 148
Ruziczka, 23, 24, 32

Salieri, A., 13, 21, 22, 23, 24,
  39, 42
Schechner, 90
Schindler, 67
Schlösser, 62

Schober, F., 49, 51, 58, 59, 71,
  78-79, 86, 97, 109, 157, 159
Schoolmaster (Schubert's
  father)—
    character of, 15-17
    marries, 15
    remarries, 16
    expels Franz, 30
    forgives Franz, 31
    buys Franz piano, 39
    again expels Franz, 49-50
    lends Franz money, 59
Schubert, Franz—
    born, 9
    receives first music lesson,
      18
    studies with Holzer, 18
    enters Convict, 19
    letter to Ferdinand, 24
    forbidden to visit home, 29
    mother dies, 31
    reconciled with father, 32
    enters St. Anna College, 33
    enters Saülengasse School,
      35
    falls in love with Theresa
      Grob, 43
    applies for post at Laubach,
      43
    leaves home, 58
    goes to Zelécz, 59
    incident with Count
      Stefan, 62
    lives with Mayrhofer, 63
    The Twins produced, 64
    dedicates Variations to
      Beethoven, 67
    and Ludlam's Cave, 68-71
    Zauberharfe produced, 71
    enters General Hospital, 73

Schubert Franz—*contd.*
   writes to Kupelwieser, 75
   composes *Schöne Müllerin*
      cycle, 78-79
   diary quoted, 76
   falls in love with Caroline
      Esterhazy, 81-82
   incident with musicians,
      83-84
   at Moonshine House, 86-87
   tours Upper Austria, 87
   and Traweger's son, 87-88
   and Weber, 89
   applies for Conductor-
      ship, 90
   visits dying Beethoven, 153
   at Beethoven's funeral,
      153-154
   at Frölichs' again, 154
   composes *Winterreise*, 154
   at Blue Hedgehog, 155
   compared with Beethoven,
      156
   goes to Ferdinand's house,
      158
   typhus becomes apparent,
      159-160
   death, 161-162
Schubert, Ferdinand, 37, 88,
      158, 160, 161
Schubert, Ignaz, 15, 35, 36
Schwind, 86, 153
Senn, 54
Sonata form. *See* Glossary
Sonatas of Schubert—
   three periods in composition
      of, 112-113
   unfinished, in C major (1815),
      113
   B major, opus 147, 59, 116

Sonatas of Schubert—*contd.*
   E♭ major, opus 122, 56, 59,
      114, 115
   A minor, opus 164, 114, 117,
      118
   A minor, opus 143, 121, 122
   A minor, opus 120, 122-123
   unfinished, in C major (1825),
      124, 147
   A minor, opus 42, 114-115,
      132
   D major, opus 53, 129, 147
   G major, opus 78, 124-126
   C minor, posthumous, 133
   A major, posthumous, 136
   B♭ major, posthumous, 138
Songs of Schubert, 56
   Abendbildern, 107
   An die Musik, 97, 99
   An den Mond in einer
      Herbstnacht, 106
   Auf dem Wasser, 107
   Das Lied im Grünen, 107
   Des Fischers Liebesglück, 107
   Diana, Der Zürnenden, 99
   Doppelgänger, Der, 108
   Drang in die Ferne, 102
   Einsamkeit, 98, 106
   Erlking, 47, 48, 58, 67, 94
   Ganymed, 106
   Gretchen am Spinnrade, 46,
      93, 94
   Heliopolis (II), 100
   Lindenbaum, 107
   Memnon, 96, 97, 98
   Nachthymne, 107
   Nonne, Der Junge, 103
   Schlaflied, 106
   Schöne Müllerin, Die, cycle,
      78-79, 102, 107

Songs of Schubert—*contd.*
  Schwanengesang, 109, 158
  Wanderers Nachtlied, 101,
    107
  Winterreise, 103, 104, 106,
    110, 154, 159
  Zwerg, Der, 80
Spaun, Josef, 25, 49, 59, 105,
  153, 159
Spaun, Max, 24, 27, 29
Stefan, Count, 61, 62, 63
Symphonies of Schubert—
  early symphonies, 46, 141
  Symphony No. 4 (Tragic),
    142, 146
  Symphony No. 5 in B♭, 47,
    141-142
  Unfinished symphony, 110,
    121, 142, 143, 144, 156
  Symphony in C major, 97,
    110, 148, 149, 155, 156

Taverns—
  Black Cat, 65
  Blue Hedgehog, 155-157
  Flying Horse, 68
  Little Flowering Plant, 68,
    69, 70
  Oak Tree, 154
  Red Hedgehog, 157
  Snail, 65
Titian's Leda, 10

Vogl, 33, 47, 58, 64, 66, 87, 153

Wanderer Fantasia, 95, 118,
  128
Watteroth, 51
Weber, C. M. von, 56, 69, 77,
  89, 155

Zauberharfe produced, 71
Zumsteeg, 28

SHORT BIOGRAPHIES

5s. each

'Each separate volume is admirably produced, sensibly bound and illustrated, and available for the very moderate price of five shillings. As a publishing venture this series deserves unstinted praise. I urge all those who are as yet unacquainted with it to lose no time in repairing their omission. The Peter Davies series should become a popular habit.'

HAROLD NICOLSON in *The New Statesman and Nation*.

'Mr. Peter Davies has managed to do what no creator of a series of small biographies has succeeded in doing before— he has persuaded his authors to be authentic biographers without any nonsense. . . . In appearance and price these volumes are perfect.' HUGH WALPOLE.

'Apart from the matter of the volumes, which in every case is from an authoritative pen, this series is a thing of real beauty. The race of people cannot yet be quite extinct who love to handle and to look at books that are seemly, books which by their very outside appearance seem to pay respect at once to the business of a writer and to the business of a publisher.' *The British Weekly*.

JULIUS CAESAR By JOHN BUCHAN

'. . . nothing but praise is due to the candour, the sustained and balanced energy, and the dramatic skill of the book as a whole . . . it is hard to conceive a better presentation of a great historical subject within the limits of a short monograph.'
The Scotsman.

' Mr. Buchan tells his famous story tersely and well . . . he has given us, within a brief compass and in language which . . . is always vigorous and effective, an admirable bird's-eye view of a truly amazing career.'

E. E. KELLETT in *The Spectator*.

VOLTAIRE By ANDRÉ MAUROIS

' . . . light and well balanced, amusing and instructive.'

DESMOND MACCARTHY in *The Sunday Times*.

' A picture of Voltaire far more vivid than many a full-length biography.' *The Listener*.

MARLBOROUGH By The Hon. Sir JOHN FORTESCUE

' The narrative of the famous campaigns is such as one would expect from so accomplished a military historian. Clear and concise in style, and necessarily compressed in matter, it gives none the less a vivid picture.' *The Spectator*.

' Seldom have an author and a subject been better fitted to each other.' *The Glasgow Herald*.

MOZART By SACHEVERELL SITWELL

' Mr. Sitwell's book is admirable. No one has brought out more clearly the inner tragedy of Mozart's life.'

The Times.

' Mr. Sitwell's eager and breathless delight quickens our nerves like a glass of wine.'

CONSTANT LAMBERT in *The Referee*.

AKBAR By LAURENCE BINYON

' The insight of the poet and the knowledge of the Orientalist are most happily blended, and the reader will here find the most vivid portrait of the great Mogul Emperor that has yet been drawn in English.' *The Times Literary Supplement*.

'The result has been a really valuable contribution to Indian history . . . Mr. Binyon's charming style and his remarkable insight into the character of his hero.'

SIR DENISON ROSS in The Observer.

LENIN By JAMES MAXTON

'Its merits are real and by no means only literary . . . there is something stimulating in the presentation.'

The Times Literary Supplement.

'It furnishes an admirable account of Lenin's life and of the development of his ideas. It does more than this . . . it supplies a very clear and intelligent outline of the history of the Russian revolution.'

MICHAEL FARBMAN in The Week End Review.

ST. PAUL By WILFRED KNOX

'Has all that effect of a sensational revelation which always comes from treating a Biblical character like an ordinary historical personage.'

CLENNELL WILKINSON in The London Mercury.

'Mr. Knox treats his subject with admirable lucidity and breadth. . . . This is a memorable and fascinating volume.'

The Manchester Evening News.

LEONARDO DA VINCI By CLIFFORD BAX

'Its mysterious and fascinating subject emerges as fascinating and almost as mysterious as before—which is quite as it should be.' SYLVIA LYND in Harper's Bazaar.

'It is the merit of Mr. Clifford Bax's sketch that it attempts to reconstruct from the multitude of data a convincing figure of a great man.' The Observer.

QUEEN ELIZABETH   By Mona Wilson

'Miss Wilson's purpose was not to re-write the history of the reign, but to recall the high purpose and vivid personality of the great Queen ; that she has done admirably.'

The Times Literary Supplement.

'This is, no doubt of it, a book that was wanted. It is brief and knowledgeable, and it allows contemporaries to speak for themselves.'

Helen Simpson in *The Review of Reviews.*

RUSKIN   By David Larg

'The most piquant biography of a great Victorian that has been published since Lytton Strachey first invented the genre. Not that justice could be done to Mr. Larg's art by describing him as an imitator of Strachey ; he is much more than that.'   *The Manchester Guardian.*

'How it all happened is told by Mr. Larg in a mosaic of intimations drawn with admirable cunning from the vast quarries of Ruskin's work . . . this admirable dramatisation and condensation, which leaves one eager to read more of what Mr. Larg can do.'   Rebecca West in *The Daily Telegraph.*

THE KING OF ROME   By R. McNair Wilson

'Mr. McNair Wilson's short but attractive study of the Napoleon who never reigned.'   *The Scotsman.*

'. . . a poignant picture of the ill-fated Napoleon's ill-fated son, a human story written with sympathy and under-standing.'   *The Manchester Evening News.*

WILLIAM OF ORANGE   By G. J. Renier

'Dr. Renier has written a brilliant but impartial sketch of a singular and arresting personality.'   *The Scotsman.*

'Dr. Renier's book should long remain the standard English life of William of Orange . . . it has struck a perfect balance between impressionism and compilation.'

The Birmingham Post.

PRINCE CHARLIE   By COMPTON MACKENZIE

'A gem (that is, it has the beauty, the scale, and the inspiration of a fine intaglio).'

OSBERT BURDETT in *John o' London's Weekly.*

'It is, of course, beautifully written . . . Mr. Mackenzie has told it finely and in beautiful proportion.'

The Glasgow Evening News.

SOCRATES   By Professor A. E. TAYLOR

'Professor Taylor tells that story . . . with the ability and knowledge which may be expected from so distinguished a philosopher and scholar.'

HAROLD DALE in *The Sunday Times.*

'Into less than 200 pages, a couple of hours' easy reading, Professor Taylor has compressed a masterpiece of portraiture and of philosophical exposition. No living English teacher of philosophy has a better command of words that convey his meaning.'

The Scotsman.

MACAULAY   By ARTHUR BRYANT

'This little biography is a skilful condensation of and selection from a great mass of material, and a just and lively presentation of the results of much study.'

ROSE MACAULAY in *The New Statesman and Nation.*

'Within its necessarily brief compass, Mr. Bryant has written an attractive, informed and sympathetic biography.'

The Week End Review.

M

MARK TWAIN By Stephen Leacock

' Mr. Leacock should convince his readers there is room for yet another book about the much be-written Mark Twain— at any rate with himself to write it.' *The Times*.

' It would be difficult to imagine a better equipped and more completely satisfying critic and biographer of Mark Twain than Stephen Leacock—the one man of this day worthy to wear Mark Twain's mantle.' *The Morning Post*.

GIBBON By G. M. Young

' It is not only that the picture of the man at all stages of life is so vivid and amusing, but that it discloses such varied erudition, such balance of judgment, such penetration of thought.' J. C. Squire in *The Daily Telegraph*.

' Mr. Young brought an already well-stored memory to his subject, as well as excellent judgment. His work is consequently of durable value.'
Desmond MacCarthy in *The Sunday Times*.

WESLEY By James Laver

' It is a serious and a sympathetic study of that burning life-long mission of the strenuous evangelist.'
J. C. Squire in *The Daily Telegraph*.

' . . . an admirable study of the man ; it is sympathetic, intelligent, and so written that the reader with little knowledge of theological or ecclesiastical problems can understand Wesley's work.' Richard Sunne in *Time and Tide*.

ST. AUGUSTINE By Rebecca West

' It is supremely invigorating to discover . . . a biography so bold, so pure, so richly garnished with observation and wise comment, as the life of St. Augustine by Rebecca West.'
Lorna Rea in *The Daily Telegraph*.

' She has penetrated into the inner life of the great African Father with an insight as rare as it is accurate ; and for Augustine's background she has given a vivid picture of the Roman world.'

The Times Literary Supplement.

CECIL RHODES By WILLIAM PLOMER

' Mr. Plomer writes trenchantly as an intelligent man of to-day ; . . . We feel a mind working all the time.'

BONAMY DOBRÉE in *The New English Weekly.*

' It is terse, well-proportioned, and spirited.'

The Spectator.

CASANOVA By BONAMY DOBRÉE

' Mr. Dobrée . . . has done his work excellently, and in good prose.' J. C. SQUIRE in *The Sunday Times.*

' Casanova is at his best in Mr. Dobrée's pages : he lends him a glamour which it is not so easy to find in his auto-biography.' *The Saturday Review.*

OSCAR WILDE By G. J. RENIER

' I believe it to be the best volume yet in this excellent series. It is pre-eminently sane, just, and charitable. It is written by a man of good taste who is also a man of the world.. The prose is simple and direct.'

COMPTON MACKENZIE in *The Daily Mail.*

' His account of Wilde's life and trial is admirable in its brevity, directness, and discretion.'

The New Statesman and Nation.

MARY QUEEN OF SCOTS By ERIC LINKLATER

' Mr. Linklater has cut straight to the heart of the problem ; he has also given us a new and reasonable interpretation of Mary's character ; and he has done all this in a hundred and fifty pages without sacrificing grace and wit of presentation. It is an admirable feat.'

EDWIN MUIR in *The Spectator*.

' Mr. Linklater can make history live. His style is so lively, his portraiture so vivid. . . .'

CAMPBELL DIXON in *The Daily Telegraph*.

RICHARD CŒUR DE LION

By CLENNELL WILKINSON

' He has succeeded in giving us an admirable, life-like portrait of a great man of action.'

R. STRACHEY in *The New Statesman and Nation*.

' Mr. Wilkinson has succeeded in giving us the soul of a man and the portrait of an epoch.'

SIR JOHN SQUIRE in *The Sunday Times*.

WILLIAM THE CONQUEROR

By HILAIRE BELLOC

' . . . brilliantly told, with that taut simplicity which is Mr. Belloc's narrative style at its best.'

JOHN BUCHAN in *The Spectator*.

' Mr. Belloc . . . was obviously the right man to add William the Conqueror to this series of short lives of great men. The choice has certainly been justified.'

The Saturday Review.

HARUN AL RASHID   By H. ST. JOHN PHILBY

' . . . What Mr. Philby has set out to do he has done admirably.'   Sir E. DENISON ROSS in *The Sunday Times*.

' This compact volume is an ornament to a fine series, and well deserves its place on the shelf alongside Mr. Laurence Binyon's *Akbar*.'   A. T. WILSON in *The Spectator*.

QUEEN VICTORIA   By Mona Wilson

' . . . an interpretation of Queen Victoria which is in-
geniously shrewd and written with distinction.'

The Daily Telegraph.

' Miss Wilson's short biography is vivacious and satisfying,
and gathers a momentum of conviction as it goes on.'

The Spectator.

SARAH BERNHARDT   By Maurice Baring

' He does it so well that we almost seem to see and hear her
still.'   *The Times Literary Supplement.*

' Mr. Baring is carrying me off my feet. . . . But what a
perfect piece of writing ! '

A. G. Macdonell in *The Bystander.*

HENRY VIII.   By Helen Simpson

' Admirers of her work as a novelist will know that they can
expect from Miss Simpson as a biographer fine qualities of
style and attack.'   *Sunday Times.*

' This is a good book, sane, scholarly and just; a little
masterpiece of compression and proportion.' *Morning Post.*

PETER DAVIES LIMITED
30 Henrietta Street, London. W.C. 2